To Pat
May God bless you
From May.

# Montego May

The Story of a Young Girl in Jamaica Growing
from a Small Girl in to Womanhood

## Lilly May

authorHOUSE®

AuthorHouse™ UK
1663 Liberty Drive
Bloomington, IN 47403 USA
www.authorhouse.co.uk
Phone: 0800.197.4150

Published by AuthorHouse 06/26/2017

ISBN: 978-1-5246-8018-3 (sc)
ISBN: 978-1-5246-8022-0 (e)

Print information available on the last page.

This book is printed on acid-free paper.

# *Contents*

# *Introduction*

I now know the hardest part of writing a book is the beginning. Where do I start? What do I say? What to put in? What to leave out? Who, if anyone will want to read it? I ask myself. Can I even be presumptuous enough to think that you would want to read about the childhood and beyond, of a very ordinary Jamaican girl?

To this I blame my confused state of mind to my many friends and my very loyal husband. Over a period of years they have been saying "Oh May" (That's me) "You must put your experiences on paper. The stories you tell, are quite intriguing and what a great record you have of your earlier years"

Why me? I say again, I'm only a very ordinary person. Although, I must confess people do tend to listen intently, when I am relating some childhood tale.

What I do know, on looking back to my very early years in that sunny Caribbean island of Jamaica were so different from the war weary European children of the 1940's?

To me, Jamaica was a land of eternal summers where children's laughter filled the air. The hum of bees and the scent of hibiscus would be all around me. Clear cool water's would be bubbling over pebble bottomed streams, And above, the palm fronds of the swaying coconut trees caught the balmy breezes that wafted on the light air. It was a land of blue skies and running waters. I know now where the word 'Jamaica' comes from. 'Xciama' which was the indigenous Arawak Indian name for "Land of wood and running Water"

It was a place of well being and tomorrow would always come. We never gave a though about our meals for they always just seemed to be there. A land where families were big and the smiles were even broader. But to this land of delight, this paradise on earth there was an uglier and darker side as you may read. And I had to change some of the names so as to avoid embarrassment to them, or their families. And so I begin my story, my thoughts put to paper and possible not the best of structured English but written in a free hand and with some of the local and colourful patois of the island as thoughts come tumbling from my head.

o-o-o-o-o-o-o-o-o-o-o-o-o-o-o-o-o-o-o-o-o

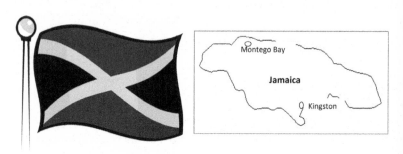

Lilly May. Nee Kerr Born. Montego
Bay 14th December 1938
Jamaica. West Indies.

(Because of an official administration error all official documents
Are dated 30th December 1938)

# Chapter 1

# *The early years*

My memory takes me back to my very young childhood and was still living with my mother. I recall an incident that happened in my neighbour's garden. I was playing with my brothers and sister and a few older friends. It was a day that was to have started a big change in my childlike life. While playing and watching the older children digging with what I discovered later was called a 'Hoe'. I tried to copy what the older ones were doing. I picked up this very heavy instrument, balanced it under one arm and with a sudden pitch forward brought it down on my brother's head. Who was kneeling down at the time? With cries of horror from the others, I looked up to see blood coming down from his scalp. In a short time my friends fetch a very gentle plump lady who took my brother by the hand and without a word took him back into the direction she came. To me, that heavy stick had become a monster which I quickly dropped and ran after my playmates who had followed the lady in to the house.

My brother was already lying on a white towel on the bed and had been seen to by our mother. Still nothing was said to me, and after a short while the whole thing was forgotten. Again I remember another incident in the same garden. I fell in to a ditch; once more this gentle plump lady was brought over. I lay in the ditch crying and nursing a heavily bleeding shin. Then the lady (my mother) knelt down and she seemed larger than anyone I had seen before. She lifted me out of a very frightening situation and cleaned up a nasty wound. She seemed such a calm and peaceful person who I saw for only a short time. Later she was taken by men in uniform (Porters) in an ambulance and I was never to see that gentle soul again. That memory still lives with me now.

Sundays in Jamaica were very noticeable. There was certain calm and peace over the island and perhaps it was a Sunday when a figure come up the path that lead to our little house. I recognised my very kind uncle who bring sweets always in a brown paper bag, of mint balls, candies and lollypops. I soon discovered that I was the favourite among the others because I was the first girl child of my mother. On that particular day, my uncle still brought sweets but there was no fun in his greeting and only a look of sadness. He said to me "Your mother won't be coming back". I did not know what else was said because my mind was anxiously taken up with this brown bag waiting to be open. I heard talking behind me and look around to see my father talking to my brothers. He then came to me and said in a very frightening voice "Your mother is dead". I do not recall ever having heard that word before and it sounded terrible. So I started to cry. It wasn't long after that my uncle left for Montego Bay where he lived. Also my father, he too worked and lived in 'Mo' Bay' (The local dialect for Montego Bay) at the Sugar Estate and only come home occasionally. From that day on I never saw my father again until what seem a long time later. I think the neighbours help to look after us (Which was the custom in Jamaica) until one day my uncle came on his way from work at the railway. Collected me and took me about two miles to meet his workmates who were waiting on the railway push trolley (A 'push me pull you' sort of trolley which were used by the workers for maintaining the tracks) and by cranking the handles up and down they pushed and pulled us all the way to Montego Bay some five miles, (8. kilometres) away. The story was said, that my father spoke to the family, saying he could not take care of five 'Pikney's (Jamaica slang for children) So after the funeral' he stay away. I was the lucky one, for I had lots of people to love and care for me. My poor brothers and sister were left behind. As I have already said, my uncle worked on the railway and I was told that he got me up at 5am every morning so he could bathe and feed me. I was also told that he would be reluctant to go to work. many times he reach the gates, he would turn around and come back to love me, and many times with tear in his eyes. Uncle lived in a bachelor's pad of a one room house. The Kitchen, Shower Room and Toilet were a little way from the place. These facilities were used by all the neighbours in the community yard. We were in fact like one big family, everyone help each other. There were times when uncle had to work a little later than 5pm. And there would be between five and six different dinners on our table all covered over from the heat, dust and flies. Those bringing the meals would say "Mr Kerr is late! Eat dis (this) chile (child)" But I would wait and fret the whole time until I see this healthy brown skin man walk through the gates. I would run and ask "Wha' you bring fi me" (for me)? His reply would generally be)

"Laud wait na". (Lord, wait a little!) Smiling broadly Uncle would inspect the different dishes and ask who had brought them? He would then set to and start the evening meal. My treats would be Sugar Cane (from the fields) or Nesberries a sweet and lovely soft fruit, Guava or June Plums. I was too young to be sent to the shops, so I would go with him. He liked good quality food and was very particular who he eat from. I liked bread and meat and he would get cross, for he believed in Vegetables, Fish and Meat as a good eating habit and plenty of fresh fruit (Which I still continue to this day) He was a very hard working man but nature told him to slow down a little, He took ill with pneumonia and was admitted to hospital. I was then taken to my Aunties house about half a mile away and soon I was joined by my little sister called Gloria. Aunty and her husband worked so we were seen to by the neighbours. She would feed us before leaving for her little café in the local market. And was a well known figure not only for her size but her temper, and was easily rubbed up the wrong way. One afternoon I remember my sister and I were sitting on a mat in the yard. My father arrived without smiles, sweets or gifts unlike my uncle. Most noticeable was the lack of love and warmth for his children, even after not seeing them for such a long time. The neighbours and he had harsh words and he walk away with my little sister who I believe was about two years old. We never saw her again until sixteen years later which will come further on in my story.

For a long time there was no news or sightings of her, and my father was asked by people who knew what he had done, Where had she gone? And also by my uncle where was little Gloria? His reply was "It's my daughter" (In other words.

mind your own damn business) For days I sat alone on the mat and longed for my little playmate. I can not remember us running about much. It seemed we were little angels always sitting down and too frightened to move. Most of the time we were too late to go to the toilet, which was in the yard. For one thing I was terrified of the noise when the chain was pulled. So I held on and held on until it was too late. Then I was punished with a beating for wetting myself. Thank God my uncle returned from hospital. This was only brought to my notice when he came in very upset and telling my Aunty "I will kill you as God made Moses if you beat Lilly May again. Since I have come out of hospital I have been getting news that the child keep crying." I overheard my Auntie's husband say. "He means every word, give the Pikney (child) back to him." I went back to my uncle, but it was not long before he was back in hospital and I was taken to by another lady who was known as Miss Mabel. Her place was about a quarter of a mile in the other direction from my Auntie's. It was a little one room building but had a nice long veranda, typical of the old Jamaican style houses and was close to the road. People passing by, would give me pennies and half pennies, and I would run inside and give them to Miss Mabel or her husband. After a short time they gave me a little box made of wood with a narrow opening at the top. They told me it was a 'Money Box' which I kept at the foot of my little bed.

There were some children next door, but they were very big and went to school. One day I was allowed to cross the 'yard' (Jamaican slang for garden or grounds) and play with them. They gave me a handful of pretty coloured things to eat. And told me to "eat them all up" As I was still a very small girl and very trusting I popped them all in to my mouth. And what a burning sensation I experienced. Oh! The pain and the agony I felt. I was on fire I was going to die! Instead of crying out I was held by these children. Their hands across my mouth and were trying to stop me from screaming. I found out much later that they had given me 'Birds Pepper' and any Jamaican will tell you they are VERY VERY HOT. It seemed a long time later before my mouth cooled down and I could talk again.

# CHAPTER 2

## *The false Teeth man*

The time came when Miss Mabel got a little fed up with me, and she sent me to the shops on the main road near where my uncle live. Now he would never allow me to go out of the gate and never on the road. This particular day she sent me to the shops to buy some green bananas. A man walking by suddenly pushed his false teeth out at me. I didn't know what they were, and thought his face had caved in. I was petrified. I ran and ran, swerving between cars, carts and bicycles down this busy road.

Eventually out of breath I slow up to see lots of 'Higgler ladies' (In English it would be 'Hagglers') Ladies selling things on the road side. They sell you things like, sweets, 'Snowballs' (which was sheared ice with syrup) If you wanted 'Back and Front' then ice cream was added to this tempting glass of delights. There were Peanuts, Coconut Water, Oranges, Sweet Potatoes and other 'Goodies' were on their carts or laid out on a blanket. I walked up to a lady; and I ask "If you could sell me some green bananas for Miss Mabel?" "Wha" she cried "Why De big people can't get de

7

bananas and de umman (Woman) sen (send) yuh (you) a Lille Pikney (Little child) for it"? I was near to tears because I had to go back and tell Miss Mabel there were no bananas. Horror! The man with the caved in face (false teeth) was still at the fence. So I waited and waited. Then he went in or so I thought, but he had only bent down. As I creep near his gate, he stand up and grinned at me. I ran off with full speed up the hill to Miss Mabel's house, Out of breath again I said "The lady says nobody can get bananas" To my dismay, she told me to go back and try further around the corner. I had to pass the 'False Teeth' man again. With shaking knees and pumping heart I made a run for it past the fence. I knew Uncle lived only up the road from the 'Higglers' (Hagglers) So I decide to see if he was out of hospital and he could get the bananas for me. 'Praise be to God' Uncle was at home and was shocked to see me, such a tiny little girl and out on her own. It was getting late and I explained why I was there to see him. His big brown hand reached down to mine and we both went to look for Miss Mabel's precious bananas. Uncle had already told me there were none to be had anywhere and I could tell he was hurt. He took me back to his house and said "Stay here" and off he went back down the road to Miss Mabel's place and was gone a long time. While waiting I thought long and hard about my dear money box which was full, and resting at the foot of my bed and I knew I would never see it again.

Back with uncle, life returned to the routine I knew. Up at five am, Bath and fed. Left with the neighbours to see to my little needs and I was loved by all. It seemed I was a happy child but really I had very little to be happy about, having no mother or father.

As time went on I started running about the yard more. I did not have to sit on the mat without moving and I was gaining a little more confidence and found a little more freedom. Uncle started sewing dresses and panties for me and every day he would plat my hair. It isn't easy combing West Indian Hair and there were always tears until the ordeal was over.

# CHAPTER 3

## *Early days at school.*

School! Oh what a lovely word! I was taken down the road, just down around the corner where my uncle took me to find the green bananas. There was a very old lady called Miss Tiny who ran a Kindergarten at a cost of 3 pence a week. (Roughly 1½p in today's money) She taught us nursery rhymes, to sing and say our times table and after a short time I was allowed to make my own way home.

The time came when I had to attend the primary school (That was free) which was not very far away and you could hear the school bell from our house during the day.

My uncle, he took time off work to get me registered. On reaching the school I was overcome by the noise and so many children, I was very nervous. The teacher had a belt that she used frequently on a child who she thought was behaving naughty. It was very hard being good, but the threat of the belt did much to curb our natural childish energy. During play time we were given a cup of milk but only to children who looked thin and hungry. On the first day my milk was taken away because I supposed I looked well covered and healthy. I was so disappointed, because with the milk, they were given a pink powder and sugar to mix with it. Sometime later I hear about a school at the Church and that was only a short distance from our yard. In fact I could see the gates of the Army Hall from where we lived. I begged and begged my Uncle to let me go to the Church School and at last he said I could go. And he was back to paying 3 Pence a week for my schooling. (Which for him, was a small sacrifice out of his railway wages) I had never gone to the Church Hall before, but would see the Church Bandsmen and followers marching past our house every Sunday evening, and just up the road they would stop outside a Chinese type of shop and have what they called 'An Open Air Meeting'. There they seemed to collect twice as many people who had been following them and then march off to the hall for another meeting. I liked the playing and the singing which was always cheerful. I wasn't allowed to stand with the Open Air Meetings as I was forbidden to leave the gate.

In the cool of the evenings after evening meals and everything was cleared away, people would sit outside on a chairs or stools and pass the time talking away the day's events. I remember one incident clearly. Doctor and Mrs Eldermeyer (they were white Jamaicans) owned the property next door to our house. They owned a lot of property, and were building a new theatre next to where we live. There were lots of comings and goings as the builders started on the foundations of what was to be 'The Roxy Theatre'. I did something stupid by running across the yard where the digging was. Then I was pulled up by what was a very sharp pain. A nail, what was called a 'Ten penny Nail' had driven in to my foot. We did not wear shoes to play in those days.

Shoes was going to special places like weddings, birthday parties or church. As I did not go to any of these special places my one pair of 'Pumps' (plimsoll's) or 'crepes' as we called them, was for school. I used to save my 'crepes' by running around in bare feet, because it was some how faster. Many a time a piece of glass or sharp stone would come to greet your unprotected feet. Not counting in later years when I would loose my toenails and lay crying in pain with the nail sticking up and the toe throbbing in pain. After the 'ten penny nail' went in to my foot, Mrs Eldermeyer got to hear about it and called to see me. Oh! I was so excited to think that a pretty lady wanted to hear that I was all right.

And so the day came when I went to the Church Primary School. I could count, say a few nursery rhymes, and pick a few words out of the reading books.

To me, the Old Hall was a big place and had lots of classes going on at the same time. I was placed in a class with a lady called Miss Campbell (Pansy, as we were to know her in later years) My mind was active and I was beginning to hold more, and could go home and constantly repeat the day's events and what I had learnt. My uncle was not sure about the Church and was not very encouraging in my progress. Another sad day came when he told me I would have to go back to the local government school, because the government 'say so'? Quite honestly I think he did not want me to get too involved with Army matters and I do not think he could carry on paying the 3 pence a week. I told Miss Campbell I could not come back and have to go to the Barrack School, and I left with a heavy heart. I was placed back in my old class that I had left what seemed only a short time ago. It was Harvest time so it must have been the beginning of a new September term. That afternoon in the shade of a large Mango Tree I remember, our class had a 'Magic Man' who pulled lots of pretty paper out of his mouth and I was frightened. We had a Harvest Service and the children took their baskets of fruit vegetables and lots of sugar cane forward to the teacher. After that, we had prayers and were allowed to go home. Learning was very slow for me, I was not settled and after school, I would wish I was going home to a mother, like every one else. When I reached home in the evenings I was called by everybody to run errands. Sometimes I liked going, other times I sulked. I did not always have a reading book of my own and could not progress in reading. I had no help with simple sums or anything. Sometimes I would ask a friend to lend me their reading book. Uncle was a wonderful man but maybe if he was married, it would have been better for me as I would have had a lady to help me read, write and do home work. After the evening meals the sun would set very quickly and our house would become quite dark. We had no electricity just a glass lamp run on kerosene oil. No sooner had we finished our meals, Uncles friends would arrive for their ritual game of cards or dominoes which went on for hours and hours. I had to get out of the way and let the grown ups get on with their gambling. I could not go to bed as we only had the one room. I felt very uncomfortable with all these men in the house with the 'cussin' and swearin' that went on. So for hours and hours I would sit on the steps out side wishing for them to go and feeling very tired. I developed 'common sense' at a very early age and I can honestly say, it isn't education that has got me through life but plenty of practical judgement, gained from having to grow up quickly. I do have my weaknesses and sometimes get a little down hearted about my limited academic abilities. But having experienced life to the full, I can move with ease amongst the 'Upper Class' and ordinary folks, as we are all equal in the sight of God.

Time move on, and I was told that I would be going to the Junior School. I was excited not because I was bright academically, but I could not stay at the Infants school for ever. It was a sign that I was slowly growing up. The whole class moved across the school yard (Jamaican for 'Grounds') to a very big building with long and wide sweeping steps leading up to the front entrance in grand colonial style. My teacher was a tall and good looking woman who looked so sweet and innocent. Until you overheard the private conversations of the 'Grown Up's' when they thought you were not around. She was known to sing like an angel in the Presbyterian Church on Sundays, but during the week, she was for the men. What a pity I heard these stories because maybe I did not listen to her as I should have. Not long after we moved to a higher class with the rest of the children. I started to make lots of friends and was very popular with our little 'Rounder's Team' I could hit the ball well with my fists (We did not use bats in those days) I loved school but hated the term breaks and often went to see if I would meet any of my friends running about the school yard. Mind you, we had to keep a watchful eye out for the school caretaker for he was known to be very mean, and would chase you off the premises. In the yard were two mango trees, and I had great pleasure in finding stones of good shape and weight and by throwing the stone at the fruit I would bring the them down. I became a very good shot and tasted many juicy ripe and plump mangos from those trees. I could only do it when the caretaker was not around. As I was growing older I was not quite so restricted as before, and could go out and play. My friends and I would go to the beach (Which was not far away) and we looked for what you call 'Mother in laws Tongue' which grew along the sea shore in between the palm trees. We would set to and make whips, by wetting the long spiky leaves then beating them with stone, we would wring out the water with our hands so it became long and pliable. We would plat the leaves together (The longer the better) and we would have our whip. By flicking our wrists up and down with whip in hand we could produce a really loud "CER-AAAACK" and we would pride ourselves on making the loudest noise from the whips we had made.

# CHAPTER 4

## Baby Sitting and Jamaican Christmas

Six weeks school holidays were much too long for me but I had 'Blossom' who was my little friend. She was the Land Lady's granddaughter and perhaps just a little spoilt, and had everything she wanted, but to me she was my friend who lived in the 'Big House', who I felt I should obey. Blossom's mother had a new baby who they called Barrington. A really lovely child and I was allowed to help walk him in the cool of a Jamaican morning which would have been around five or six am. There was Blossom's mother, Blossom and I with Barrington (Barry) in his buggy which was sent specially for him from America, we would stroll the early morning in the quiet streets of Montego Bay. (How easy it was to get up those days) Blossom's mother was a kind lady and many times would give me little gifts. I think she felt sorry for me. At Christmas time, Blossom was the star attraction. For many of her presents were sent from America by her Grand Aunties. We were all joyful when the postman arrived with a big parcels and another time to say there was a parcel at the

16

Post Office. Christmas morning was a real eye opener. There were so many beautiful things in the boxes for Blossom, and later for Barrington. There were beautiful ribbons to china dolls. She had black patent shiny shoes with pretty socks and lots of other lovely things. After all the presents were opened and all the wrappings cleared away, the custom was throughout the island, would be time to serve up the huge traditional Christmas Breakfast. The ladies prepared and set the tables for their families. Those who did not want to use the kitchen would cook on their little stove's that burnt wood or charcoal set outside their modest little homes. Christmas Breakfast would have Jamaica Bread and best butter. There would be hard boiled eggs, Avocado Pears, Lettuce, Tomatoes, Cucumbers, Ackee and salt fish, Roast Breadfruit, fried fish with plenty of vinegar and black pepper. Hot chilli peppers with heaps of onions. Some would boil green bananas and mackerel and we would all sit down to this enormous breakfast while others in the yard would have already marinated the Christmas Days chicken or rooster, pot roast beef or pork. The Red Kidney beans would have been in water, soaking overnight for our National Jamaican dish of 'Rice and Peas' (Peas being the Kidney Beans) and this would be served up in huge quantities for our Christmas dinners.

I digress...... Back to Blossom my little friend. She chose me to comb her hair rather than her mother. If I recall, she had lovely hair, quite soft and short which needed a lot of brushing to get it together to tie the ribbons. She was allowed to go to the Christmas Morning Matinees at the Strand Theatre (Owned by the Oldemeyers) I could not go, as Uncle could not afford the ticket price. Also I had no decent clothes to wear. I always told myself that I was lucky to be living with Uncle and not with a stranger in the country parts where there were no lights, usually lonely and dark.

While I waited for Blossom to return from the matinee to tell me what went on. I was given a balloon and a penny whistle which I would play with for hours everywhere seem quiet because all the neighbouring children had gone to the show. Another thing, my friends had their hair straightened for Christmas. My Uncle did not believe in the worldly things (except gambling) He said "If God wanted you to have pretty hair he would have given you straight and pretty hair". So mine was never straightened for years. He also believed that the 'Inner Man' should be well fed. It did not matter too much about clothes. So I had one set of clothes on, and one set in the wash and that was it. His theory was 'you should not have too much of anything because when you die, you cannot take it with you'. I never felt jealous of Blossom but wished I could have had just one pair of shoes and one pretty dress.

Well Christmas, was over and life took on normal everyday routine, with people starting back to work, and us back to school. My friends would be excitedly talking about what they had for Christmas and where they went during the holidays. Some time later our teacher told us there was a show coming to the Strand Theatre and it would be educational and some of the classes from the school would be taking part. They were a percussion group, I looked forward to that day for a very long time and I was not disappointed after the long wait and much pleading with my Uncle for the money, we had to take to school in order to gain entrance to the Theatre. I struggled at school. Each day I found the work became harder. Without the help of books you can be one step behind the subject. I enjoyed spelling, reading and dictation. I was interested in stories of people in other lands, never dreaming that one day I would see and visit many of the countries we read or heard about.

Mathematics (or sums we used to say) was an issue which I never really mastered.

Our school uniform was a navy blue skirt and a white blouse. Shoes were optional, for those who could afford them. Even now I remember my first proper pair of shoes which were given to me by Miss Lucille It was an 'old –ish' brown coloured sort of boot. Most of the time our shoes were hung around our necks tied by the laces,. This was to save the wear and tear on them. Our feet got dusty and dirty but never wore out!! Actually we took great pride in our shoes. After playing all day long in the hot and dusty school grounds, we would pick hibiscus flowers from the hedges and fences from people's gardens on the way home and with the petals give our shoes a good clean. Oh they used to polish up lovely. After arriving home I would often wash my school blouse have it dried, ironed and ready to wear, smart and clean for the next day. I counted myself one of the lucky ones as I did not have to feed the goats, pigs or chickens. I did not have to do the heavy washing or scrub the floors before I left for school. But sometimes I would mop and polish the house after school had finished if I was told to, or wanted to be praised by my Uncle. In Jamaica, children were encouraged to do duties before they went to school or when they come home. At times I used to watch my friends washing large white sheets and other clothes early in the morning. They would have to make breakfast or clean the house. Then with sweat running down their faces dash off to their schools. If they lived near enough, they would have to come home during the lunch break and carry on with the cleaning, or when they arrived home in the afternoon. Some of the children were brought up by people outside of their own family. Some who were only a little better off than they were? They said, they could be given a better life. Except that they usually ended up a little more than unpaid maids or helpers. At an early age I used to feel sadness for these girls and boys who were equal to my own years. There were times when I was really grateful to my Uncle for taking me in after the death of my mother and being abandoned by my father. I used to feel very sorry and guilty for my brothers and sister and felt they were being used in the same way. They had no choice and had to be given to other people to be looked after. Occasionally I would see one of my brothers in the market, passing with whoever he was staying with. We had great big smiles for one another and ask how you are? The other would reply "Fine or great" It was not true of course because the foster parent or person, who had taken them in, was always around. It was during those times I thought of them often.

I was not the oldest child but the eldest girl. I was told in later years that Uncle spoilt me from when I was born. And he was the only one who really cared for me. I was given cuddles which were lovely but unfortunately no financial support for school.

# Meeting my father

One day he said to me "I want you to run an errand. To my surprise Uncle sent me to The Barnett Sugar Estate, that's where my father worked, He had never done that before, and I was full of doubts and anxiety as I remembered the way my father took away Gloria my little sister and never return her. Anyway, the message for my father was to ask him to give me some money for school books, as it was coming up to exam time. When I arrived at the Estate, I told the man at the gate "I come to see my father", He replied "Wah a doo yu faader" (Who is your father?) I told him Henry Pugh. I was told, he was not far away and to go on in. My father must have seem me coming because he hid round a corner, I said to two men who stood staring at me "Mi aa lookin fe missah Pugh" (I am looking for Mr Pugh) The men turned around and looked in the direction my father, and shouted "Enry! wam Pikney aa look fee yu" (Henry, a child is looking for you) My father took a long time to come out from his hiding place and I gave him the message. As he stood looking at me, one of the men asked "Aa fee yu Pikney"? (Is this your child?) When my father answered yes, the man said "Laaad yu mean yu is iding from your chyle?" (Lord you mean to say you are hiding from your child) My father gave me two shillings and sixpence which in today's money would be twelve and a half pence (or 'P' as it is commonly called), I took it home but felt really ashamed that I had to go begging to my own father. I really hoped that Uncle would not send me again but once more I had to make the trip to the Sugar Estate and the same episode took place. I came home with two shillings and sixpence. But this time when I told my Uncle he said in no uncertain terms that "I should have thrown the money in his face" I was never sent again for which I was very thankful. Now would you believe it? One day my father turn up with a man he said was his brother and he was going to take me away from Uncle. People in the yard just stood around shocked 'What a cheek' After all those years of ignoring us and leaving us. I told him I was not going, and when my Uncle came home from work he said "Over his dead body does this child leave this house" Only he used more colourful language and told him exactly where he could go, My father and his so called brother whom we had never seen before left. I was quite upset over this incident. My 'New so called Uncle' came a few times afterwards to visit me. He was so unlike my father who was very dark and this man was nearly white. Another time my father turn up with a very tall fair skinned lady from the country. They looked me over and said to tell my uncle that they would be coming to collect me the following day. Oh how I cried and cried. When my uncle came home from work, everybody was rushing from the yard to tell him what my father had said. My uncle was so sad and told me that he could not stop him taking me this time because he was my real father and to save any bloodshed he would have to let me go.

# CHAPTER 6

## *Under the bed*

I was determined I was not going. The following day the landlady's eldest granddaughter called me to the big house. She ask if I wanted to go with my father. I again said "No" She said "De ooman yu faader a bring back hah no teet! Dem false" (The lady your father is bringing back has no teeth of her own) Well I like 'Johnny Cakes' (Dumplings). And if you bite in to a Johnny Cake your teeth can come out. Everybody knew it was my weakness, and I would not be getting any more, because the lady cannot eat them, so she wouldn't make them. I still said "Mee Nah a go" (I am NOT GOING!!) Monica (the eldest granddaughter) quickly pushed me under her grandmother's bed. It was a big high four poster, with a valance down to the floor. She told me not to come out until she came for me. Later I could hear voices outside and Monica saying "She had not seen me all day" Oh I kept SO quiet even frightened to breath properly. Time passed slowly by and then at last there was peace and quiet, they were gone. Monica who we called 'sister' as a pet name came into the room stooped down by the bed and shouted "A

Yu a sleep (Are you sleeping) to which I answered "No" "Well dem come out now" (Well then come, you can come out now) I was so relieved, and my father never came back. Well that was another chapter in my young life. One day another man called to see my uncle, and they talked for a very long time. He called me to say this was a cousin of ours. He is now going to America; he has been married for a long time and his wife cannot have any children and wanted to adopt me. The man seemed friendly and kind. He told me he could give me a little more help than uncle. He told me I would have pretty frilly dresses, patent shoes and dolls. I would even have a room of my own. I said I want to stay with my uncle. I must admit I liked the man and was tempted to go, but I could not just go and leave uncle, it wouldn't have been right. The man asked if I would like him to send a doll from America. I said "No tank yu" (No thank you) He ask what I would like? I surprised myself by saying a Bible I'm sure it was an unusual request for he looked shocked and repeated "A Bible?" I said yes please. I was overjoyed and excited. Because he said he would send one. Every day I thought about that Bible and hoping when I came home from school I would find it waiting for me. Oh it was such a long time coming, the days passed slowly by and the mail box always seem empty. Then 'Praise be to God' one day I came home and there it was, waiting for me wrapped in brown paper with pretty stamps on the parcel and string around it.

I quickly opened it and there before me was the most beautiful sight. A black covered Bible. My uncle came home to find me beaming from ear to ear. He too was delighted and said, "Oh he has remembered". We both read a couple of verses from the 'Good Book'. But of course I was too young to really understand the deeper meanings. Today I still cherish and read my Bible and it travels with me wherever I go. It is well used now and has to be treated with care as it is showing age with use and constant handling. Nothing will ever replace this gift I received so many years ago. There was a chorus I used to sing as a girl which went *'My Bible and I, my Bible and I. What a wonderful treasure, God's gift without measure. We will travel together, my Bible and I'*. There was a time when I nearly lost it. Years later, our family were flying off for a holiday. We had to leave the house early and I could not find my Bible. I remember taking it to church the previous Sunday. On our way to the airport, we called in at the Church Hall. where we worshiped. It was not there, my heart sank. I was not happy and kept thinking about it whilst on holiday. On our return I was sure my Bible would have been found and set on the Hall Table, we called in, but no one had seen it. Week's later after visiting a friend and opening my heart to her about my Bible; it came to light that she had been tidying the Worship Hall and took it home for safe keeping. Even with all the announcements from the platform. It did not register that the name inside and the place where it had come from was for me (I took my Uncles Surname of 'Kerr' and the church was the Church Hall in Barnett Street 'Mo' Bay') (Slang for Montego Bay Jamaica) so it meant nothing to my friend. She had placed it on a shelf in a cupboard. Oh I was so glad that my treasured gift had come home.

# Chapter 7

## *Back of the class.*

My Uncle Joseph came to live in the same communal yard where his brother Ivan (my Uncle) or Cyril or he was better known by everyone who knew him. Uncle Joseph was not as caring as I thought he could have been. Maybe a shilling or two (5p) could have made a difference to my schooling. Times got a bit hard for my Uncle, what with the constant gambling at our house. Furniture and other household items began to disappear to the Pawn Shop, to be collected again on Pay Day. I overheard one late afternoon that the wages at the railway were paid fortnightly and he used to get £7.00. The evening following a Pay day, there was always a big meal, which most of it was given out to his friends with a few beers or rum. With nearly all of the money gone, my requests for clothes and other things were never met. Once again it was left for the next fortnightly wage. School and Exercise books were given out for free but like the school milk they dwindled away. I was now in the fourth Form and at last Uncle gave me money for a reading book. I was overjoyed. I used brown paper to cover and to protect it as I wanted it to remain new forever. My name and address were written on the front and the back. I could now read after school. Some words I had to break down to get the full understanding of what was printed, and many times I would ask someone to sit and explain my homework. How I missed my mother. There were mixtures of different abilities in the same classroom. Some were fortunate to have parents who could afford to buy books for their children. They were always put in the two front rows, nearest to the teachers. Children who could get books were in the middle rows and the less fortunate like me were always at the back. In my early days our class numbers sometimes ranged up to seventy who were controlled by two teachers? One trained and one auxiliary. For me, school days were happy days. I had lots of friends and got on well with the teachers. I was always out to please them but as I had no books, I was kept at the back of the classroom with others who were poor. They were not always pleased with me and my homework.

# CHAPTER 8

## *Fetch the belt!*

I lived about quarter of a mile (400 metres) from school and I could make this even shorter by cutting through the neighbours yard (Garden). The yards were divided either by corrugated fencing or barbed wire which sometimes would catch and tear your clothes or your hands? Uncle was a strict disciplinarian and I often had the belt for ripping my dress or breaking some household crockery, and being cheeky. Uncle would sometimes come home to a barrage of complaints from the neighbours who had ask me to run errands. I would grin and say "Why not your self go or what did your last servant die of?" Oh these were terrible things to say to a grown up in those days. And so I had to pay the penalty for my rudeness by again getting a belting.

Children had to go and fetch the belt for their punishment. I discovered it was easier to delay the beating by pretending to go for the strap, and then make a run for the gate. This would make Uncle mad and he would chase me a long way to catch me.

This would cause laughter on the street. When caught,

I would be SO sorry for myself and with tears running down my cheeks would be pleading to be let off. I would tell my Uncle how much work I would do, and when I grew up I would never leave him, and I would wash and iron his shirts. But he took no notice and would march me home! Once inside the belt would rain down on me. Oh! How it hurt! There were marks on my skin for days afterwards always itching in the heat. I would cry for what seemed hours hoping Uncle would come and cuddle me and tell me how sorry he was. Occasionally he would give me a penny to get some sweets, and in no time the crying would stop. Or he would sit and look quite upset and I would cry all the more because I was sorry for him looking at me with his big sad brown eyes. When there were no more tears I would wet my finger and with the spittle would wipe it down my face to keep my cheeks constantly wet. Or I would repeat over and over "I wish my mother was not dead" This would really hurt him, He must have been very fond of his sister. It was the normal practice in those days. Our love for our parents was no less than before the beatings My Uncle had many quotes and sayings, which at the time were not clear to me. But today when memories comes flooding back their meanings are understood and remember the truth behind what he was saying. Even today without thinking I would repeat them to my own family, a wise or well known Jamaican saying. For instance, if uncle had just been helping a neighbour he would say "Wan 'and wash de udder" (One hand washes the other) meaning, the neighbour would help you in return. Or another comes to mind when I was walking with Uncle in the country parts in the heat and along the dusty tracks. I would want to take a short cut. He would say" Short pass draw blood. Long pass draw sweat" meaning 'the long way round may take more time, but with less effort'. Another was "If Arry caan catch yuh. Dem im catch ah shirt (If the Devil can't catch you then he will catch your children) "A dog im bring ina bone anim tek one out" Meaning (If you bring in tales to the house, then you will take them out.) Oh there were many many more saying uncle used to quote to me.

Getting back to my school days, Our Headmistress was a remarkable woman who taught many of the inhabitants in 'Mo Bay' (Montego Bay and the surrounding districts) going back numerous years. Some children from outlying country parts or Fishing villages would have walked up to 7 miles (approx 11 kilometres). They arrived at school, very hot, dusty and sweaty. After school was there would have been the long walk home again. One day, the headmistress asked me if I would collect her lunch as her maid was ill. I was delighted at this honour, but after a few months of running this errand I realised I was missing a lot of the morning lessons as she lived some distance from the school. I mentioned to my uncle that I was unhappy about my school work. He wanted to know why? After explaining to him about the lunch I had to fetch every day, he said it had to stop. I told this to the headmistress who did not take kindly that I was not doing it any more. A few days later when I was working in the school garden (As part of our lessons) my hands were waving and flapping about as I was trying to get away from a wasp (believe me, Jamaican Wasps have very nasty tempers!) She saw this from her office window and summoned me to her room. She gave me no chance to explain but laid in to me with a thick leather belt saying "I was wasting time" I left her office and ran straight home still stinging and smarting from the blows I had received. Unusual for Uncle he was at home and I cried and sobbed out my story to him at the time he was playing his usual dominoes game with friends. Without a word, he gently pushed his chair back and strode to the door, newspaper firmly tucked under his arm. In the background I heard one of his friends say "Truble tu' day man, Cyril im ah gone a waar" (Watch out Cyril's on the war path). I trailed behind, wishing with all my heart I had kept my mouth shut. On arriving at school, Uncle spoke for the first time since we left home. He told me to find the Headmistress which I did. When she came out on the balcony, Uncle strode up to her, pushed his face very close to hers and said "If yu waan Pikney fee beat, go a fine a man fee give yu one" Meaning 'If you want a child to beat, go lay with a man and get your own child'. Having then made his point and marched out of the school leaving her standing there and lost for words. I slipped quickly back in to my classroom wondering what would happen to me, but I was never troubled by her again. It was not long after that incident I had the offer of a little lunch time job. There was a lady who owned a small store at the top of our street (for those who know 'Mo Bay' it was Barnett Street) She ask if I would collect her lunch from home and bring it to her at the shop and she would give me two shilling and sixpence (12.½ p) a week. I was overjoyed, I still had almost the same distance as before but the big difference was I did not have to leave class early and I was getting paid for doing it. What a joy it was to receive my first pay packet. Each week I gave the money to a kind and nice lady who lived in our yard and she would save it for me. And for the first time in my life I was able to buy Christmas presents. I brought Uncle a pair of pyjamas, a hat for me to wear at church and some materials to make a dress. Unfortunately this new found wealth was short lived as I was no longer needed, and was back to how it always had been, impoverished!! The area where I lived there were other schools Beaconsfield, Cornwall College, Mount Alverna and there were others which I would not have known about. Beaconsfield was the most coveted girl's school while Cornwall College was for the boys. Only the 'Well to do's' or clever would be accepted in to these schools. My one wish was to attend Beaconsfield but Uncle had neither the means nor me the education to get there. So my remaining time was spent at the Government School. One day, during a term break, after Uncle had gone to work. I got up but felt somehow very strange. I had vague sorts of feelings I could not shake off. I was pottering about, waiting for my friends to call, as we had planned to go to the beach. When the time came I did not want to go, and they could not understand why? To them I looked so sorrowful. While waiting for my callers, I had been singing from out of the old 'Sankey's Hymn Book' which Uncle kept over his bed on a little shelf. The songs were nice and happy, but there was one in the book I had not noticed before but had heard the 'Grown Ups' singing the words. *"Were you there when they crucified my Lord? Sometimes it causes me to tremble, yes tremble. Were you there when they crucified my Lord?"* I had never felt anything like it before, but there was a guilt I could not explain. I wept and wept what seemed for hours. The whole day I stay in the house except for once, coming to the door and finding the yard looked clean and tidy, the mango tree looked as if the leaves had been polished. I can not remember having any lunch because it seemed so sad that I had helped to kill Jesus. That must have been the beginning of my conversion and my understanding of the love of Jesus. Soon I was back at school trying to learn or catch up with my lessons. And enjoying the game I loved best. Which was 'Rounder's' during the morning or afternoon break.

# CHAPTER 9

## *From a 'Pickney to Puberty'*

Then things started to change I was beginning to get chubby and was becoming more self conscious of my body. My breasts had started to develop and to me it was a very worrying time, because I would have to ask Uncle for some money to buy a brassiere and then I would have to find a way of putting it on. There was a little shop about 3 doors away which sold panties, slips, lace and other pretty clothes. I saw hanging up a blue linen bra' going for two shilling and sixpence (12.½p). For weeks I kept my eye on it, hoping no one would buy it until I could find the courage to ask Uncle for the money to get it. To my shock, an old gentleman who every one called 'Daddy' who lived close by and we all shared the communal yard. He said "Why don't you tell your Uncle you need a Bra. You will get pains in your chest with those things bobbing about. I was so embarrassed as there were many people standing around listening.. It was then the turn of the women in the yard to draw Uncles attention that I had two jiggling lumps that needed controlling. I quickly went to my Uncle "The lady at the shop is selling a Bra for 2 shillings and six pence.(15p) But 'Daddy' who was a kind man gave me the money there and then. I ran to the shop and ask the lady to sell me the brassiere. She asked me what size? But I had no idea. She gave me the Bra wrapped up in newspaper. I ran past all the people in the yard who were looking and went to the toilet to try it on. It was Oh No! <u>too tight,</u> but I was not going to take it back, I had gone through enough humiliation for one day. Then a few days later I had my first period. Having no mother I didn't really what to do and I went through a lot of anxious and worrying days. Eventually I told a friend called Millie about what was happening to me. She told me her mother would help me. I went to her house and Millie's mum explained to me it was a normal part of growing up and my body was changing. She put like a nappy on me and I felt a little better. I don't know if Sanitary towels or Tampax had reached Jamaica yet but we used White Birds Eye Cloth. This was a white material with tiny raised bumps. They were cut in to squares then attached with bits of string long enough to go round your waist. She also gave me a little lecture on how I was not to play with boys or I will get a baby. I was very very frightened because there were lots of boys playing marbles outside the house! I looked out and wondered how I was going to get home. If I passed these boys, would I be getting a baby? Eventually the boys left. I made a dash for home and never stopped until I was safely inside our house. Then Oh my God! It suddenly came to me that Uncle was a boy, what I am going to do when he comes. It was nearly dark when he came in and I was thankful he did not have to see my face. I think looking back on the incident; he went and had a talk with my aunty about my period. And borrowed money to get Millie's mother to make me some 'nappies' because in a short time they were given to me and the whole lecture on how to wash and bleach them and how I could have a baby if I play with boys. This was sad because I liked playing marbles with the boys and the girls and until now had never given a thought about babies.

I also noticed that the girls did not stop playing with the boys like I did. Then one day a Doctor went to the school to talk to the girls. I wasn't there that day. Anyway, this talk, which was passed on, second hand, proved helpful. I discovered I could only get a baby if I did wicked and dirty things and if I did, God would punish me. I already had a few run –ins with God at school. I had had a couple of fights and told a few white lies but this new experience was Hell itself. Oh I did not want to burn in that Hell Fire, Uncle was always talking about. All I wanted was to play marbles and cards for broken plate money (that was our school girl currency) and only to skip and go on the merry go round until I was dizzy. That's all. I never was going to do that other naughty thing!!

## Chapter 10

# *The bouncing coconuts*

Another naughty thing comes to mind (Well not that naughty) but to Uncle it was shame on his name of Kerr that I went in to the house of God and misbehaved.

My friend Minerva (also known as 'Tiny') heard of a big Christian Rally in the town.

There was in a big marquee put up, and hundreds of people attended the meetings.

Singing hymns, praising God, and being spiritually uplifted only the way Jamaicans can worship. Tiny and I decided to go to one of the meetings just to see what was going on. So we went to the marquee which sort of dominated the area and slipped under the rolled up walls of the tent which helped the slightly cooler air to circulate around the crowds of people who were packed in there. Well the music was loud, the singing was louder, and the clapping and cheering was enthusiastic. "Praise the lord" were on hundreds of lips, and the preachers were in full flow. Being young and giggly we were soon laughing at the joy and dancing with some of the older and more portly members of the congregation who were taken up with the spirit of worship. We were enjoying ourselves at their antics and not realising that our laughing was being noticed by some of the elders. One who knew Uncle, slipped out of the meeting to complain about our behaviour. Well, Uncle was livid and came looking for us. The first thing we knew about this trouble is when I saw two big brown feet and legs come tramping around the side if the tent where we were standing. I recognised them straight away and said "Oh no Tiny, it's Uncle, quick lets run" and ducked out from the marquee and started to race down the street. Uncle saw us and with a shout of anger came after us. We ran like the wind and Uncle was getting further behind. The next thing we knew was a loud thumping and bumping noise was around our feet and we saw coconuts bouncing past us. Uncle in his fury got some coconuts from somewhere and was throwing them down the street after us. How we jumped, leaped skipped and hopped, dodged and swerved to miss these projectiles which were coming thick and fast. I was dreading going home that night but eventually had to go. There was Uncle fuming and had an ultimatum for me. He said he had enough of me and I had to go. So I was sent back to my real Father who lived one street away. Oh how I pleaded and cried but it was no use, I was packed off to where he lived. Even worse, the next day my Father told to me to iron trousers. I was horrified; I had never ironed anything before, and had only watched my Uncle as he did all those things. I made a proper mess of his trousers and he shouted at me and told me to do them properly as I had made about eight seams in the front of his trouser. Later when Uncle came from work I went back to him and told him about what had happened. I knew that my uncle would not have approved me using a hot iron and trying to iron trousers which I have never done before. He was very angry at my Father and told me I had better come back to him. Oh I was so pleased to be back in my own bed again and back in Uncle protective care. And I can say I never misbehaved in church again. At the age of 14, I was beginning to think what was going to happen to me when I leave school and how worried I was. Most of the children who I played with or in the neighbourhood had already left school and started sewing with a Seamstress or taken up domestic duties (A maid serving in some house). The better off or rich kids would have taken their entrance exam for Beaconsfield or Mount Al Verna colleges. I would have liked sewing but it meant a fee each week which Uncle could not afford because of his gambling and entertaining nearly every night. I certainly did not care for domestic duties and did not want to scrub other people's floors or do their washing ironing and cooking. For I had seen too many girls just a bit older than me struggling with heavy pails of water or polishing floors with the sweat running down their arms. Although still young, I had a lot of pride.

# CHAPTER II

# My first full time job

One evening a lady came to our yard to visit a friend and saw me. She asked if I would like a little job (I though it would be another errand to the shops) Then she told me a friend of hers worked at a big and well known book store in Montego Bay. This friend was going to have a baby and needed some time off. The owners had told her if she wanted her job kept, she would have to find somebody to stand in until she was ready to come back. What a joy! What a wonderful feeling. I cannot say prayer was answered because I did not pray for a job in a store. Uncle him always say "God will not walk with the proud or the scornful" I did not want God to know I was proud and scornful!! I mentioned this to Uncle one evening just before he was going to start play cards with his friends. He did not encourage me because I would have to leave school before my proper time. I only had six months before I finished anyway. I mentioned this to Uncle. His reply was "if you caan spell your name, dem no blame mi" (If you can't spell your name then don't blame me)

One Monday morning I was taken by the lady whose job I was standing in for, to Milton's Book Store, a large shop that catered for all the schools on the island. They also ran a grocery a chemist and perfumery section as well. The department I was in, sold books, pens, pencils, and toys I also had to run errands to the bank, Post office and building societies. Oh! And wash the floors every Thursday afternoon when it was half day closing in Mo'Bay. How I slaved away in that shop. Today it would be classed as child exploitation and cruelty. Later in my story I shall explain how. Mrs Milton my boss and her family who were white Jamaicans were so cruel. She had two sons and two daughters who helped with the business.

By this time I was a regular church goer and would hop from the Church to the City Mission. There use to be a youth club at the bottom of our road run by a white lady. All the young people I knew went there most nights to play records sew or cook. I was persuaded to go one night but could not settle, so I did not go again.

This constant drawing to the church was so strong it was like a drug. No sooner was one meeting over then I would be making my way to the other. I had given up most of my friends because they were not interested in church and that was where my heart was. Going home from the second meetings each night means I was tired for work the next morning. After working in the store for six months the lady had her baby and turned up to say "She would be back the following week" for her job and was promptly told they would rather keep me on. She of course was very angry with the boss. Another job was offered to her but was to be a domestic at the house where they lived. She of course refused and left cursing and shouting at them. I felt sorry for her but at the same time I don't know if I was pleased for having her job. What task masters the Milton's were, from 8am until 5.30pm I was continually on my feet. Never allowed to sit down, I stood behind the book shelves to eat my two pieces of bread and water interrupted by calls from Mrs Milton to do various jobs. For this constant taking advantage I was paid five shillings a week (in today's money it would be 25p. And so the months slipped by. There was a boy working in the next department named Vincent, one day he left and never returned and so more duties were loaded on to me.

# CHAPTER 12

## *On hands and knees*

Every Thursday afternoon I had to wash the all the floors in the store on my hands and knees throughout the entire building. I had to change the water many times because I was told to use a hand scrubbing brush. And scouring powder then rinse and dry with clean cloths. I was there for hours working in the heat of the day and feeling half dead by the time I had finished and could go home. The thought of taking a nice cool shower and then getting to my beloved church, it helped to keep me going. The people at the City Mission and the Church were kind and friendly and they knew that I was being brought up by a single man. They also knew I had no mother. But I never told anyone how desperate I was, and could do with help in many ways. Most of them thought I had all I needed, and was well behaved. Mr Kerr or Cyril (My Uncle) they would say had done a good job and his sister would have been proud of him. One day, Mrs Milton's daughter had a little talk with me and wanted to know more about my life. Told her what there was to know? She asked me about 'boy friends' and told her I did not have one as I liked going to church even better. I then became a laughing stock at work and an object to poke fun at. I couldn't do my duties as I was always at church!! Some more of the many duties I had to do was to go and fetch the lunch from Mrs Hiltons house about a mile away. Vincent was now gone and not there to carry it. Every day I had to collect this tray from the big mansion house, surrounded by small Mango and Orange trees and other fruit. Ripe Mangoes and Grapefruits used to be lying on the beautiful green and manicured lawns, only to be eaten by wasps bee's and ants. I was desperately hungry but too frightened to pick up any of the fruit in case the cook (who was very sharp and not at all friendly) would report me to the Milton's. In those days I was too proud for my own good. Every day I had to carry the hot heavy tray on my head, I could feel the heat coming through to my scalp. I would shift the tray from side to side or on to my shoulders then back on to my head. Some days I could have cried. I dreaded this extra burden placed on me; after all, I was not yet fifteen years old and I could not see a way out. My problems did not stop there.

# CHAPTER 13

## *The gambling men*

After church at night, I would come home to find a group of men with my Uncle, going at the card games as if there was no tomorrow. I would get so disheartened at times. After hearing the preaching and beautiful words of God this was the last thing I wanted to get home to. Some nights I would sit on the doorstep in the dark just waiting for the men to leave. When I came back in my Uncle would say in a loud voice "Where yu bin all de night, me a gonna knock de church out a yu head" I think you can translate that easily enough? Sometimes I would go to bed while the card players were still there. Uncle had screened off my bed with a blanket, but how could you sleep with the men swearing and drinking just a few inches (a few centimetres) from my head? These men were very respectful towards me. They would tip their hats and call me 'Miss May' or Maam. I could not fault them, Uncle would put a stop to it by reminding them "Mine de 'Pikney she inner bed" (Mind the child she is sleeping) and for a while there would be low talking but the shuffling of the cards and the clinking of the rum bottle would still be quite evident.

I dreaded going back to work in the mornings tired through lack of sleep and the heavy duties I had done the day before, Oh! Such trouble if I was a minute late. There were two of us employed in the bookstore department, myself and an elderly gentleman who had been working there for years. He had great knowledge of everything to do with the store and was very much depended upon. He went home most days for his lunch when there were not many people in the store. He had a very bad stomach, burped a lot and was sometimes doubled up in pain. I thought to myself "I'm going to be like that in a few years time from all the hard work and hardly any lunch. I did not mention this to Uncle as I had no future plans ahead but at that time I did miss school. One of Mrs Milton's sons came in to the shop most days, not to help with the work, but to help himself to money from the till and go off to the bar a few yards (Metres) down the road. I spent many trips to that bar ordered by his mother to fetch him and his brother back to the shop. The brother worked in the Chemist department and was always feeling unwell. Mrs Milton used to make him a medicinal Drink and one of my many errands was to take it to him every day. How he hated me bringing him this home made concoction and would swear at me or the drink. He had an assistant and they would whisper together every time I approached them. Then one day the assistant finally made a move and asked if I would like to go out with him for a drive in his car that night. I said "No thank you" quite bluntly. He never asked again but I could see his eyes staring and undressing me. I was nobody's fool, and no rich man was going to take advantage of me as a naive overworked teenager, and as poor as a church mouse. I heard a couple of my school friends played with boys and were now having babies! What a shock! I really did feel sorry for them. It was the first time that I heard of 'children having children' My Uncle said "God is coming soon because the Bible says in the last days; these thing will come to pass" Well I got myself an exercise book with the intention of keeping my own records. As I was continually told that God keeps a Big Black Book and he writes down everything we do or think of which is wrong, The First couple of days after recording my failures, I was telling myself I wasn't too naughty, then after a couple of days I gave up because what started out as half a page turned out to be several full pages, and I felt sure I was going to be sent to Hell. I look back now and can smile at my innocence. The only thing I was guilty of was feeling angry at the men who came with my Uncle to gamble, I really hated them for coming to our house.

I was getting more and more involved in the "City Mission Church but at the same time wanted to be at the Church. I was being pulled both ways not by people but my own feelings. Each night I sat in the City Mission behind big double doors and believed every word that was preached. After these heavy Gospel messages there would be an altar call and people would try and bring you to the Penitent Form at the front and pray with you. I used to hop outside during these times and come back in when things cooled down a bit. This was every night except Friday and Saturday evenings. One night I had a little piece of pencil in my hand and decided to write on the door (While no one was watching) 'Please God save me tonight' Anyway I still slipped out after the call to the Penitent Form. Now one night the Minister gave a powerful message and all I can remember was being taken by the hand and walking forward with the Lady Minister, Miss Patnam. She prayed and prayed for me, and it was then that I gave my heart to my best friend God. Oh! How I cried and cried, I thought I would die from exhaustion. When everything was quiet I told the minister I did not want to go home as I wanted to hang on to the feelings of joy and elation for as long as I could. Could they send word to Uncle? They took me across the church yard and to their living quarters and I spent the night on a little bed they made up But I couldn't sleep. I was worried about what Uncle would say because he did not like those sorts of churches, and I also worried that the beautiful feeling of being saved would go away. At six thirty in the morning I got up to thank Miss Patnam and went home to face whatever came. Uncle was very quiet, and I had a shower and went to work. All day I thought about the church, Tea time I got home tired as usual, but could not wait for the meeting times. I did what Uncle asked of me and then I was off to church a couple of hours early. There were two girls next door to the City Mission and they came out to talk to me, We sat on the church steps and they wanted to know how I felt, I really did feel different, a Glow deep down inside and an overwhelming love for God. I wanted to tell everyone. At last people began to arrive and the service started. We prayed and sang and then it was time for testimonies (A time when you can stand up and say what God has done for you or how you feel about him) I was first on my feet telling of the love of God. I opened my mouth as the scriptures told me and it was filled with words. I made a promise that I will never leave the Lord and that promise still holds true today.

# CHAPTER 14

## *Slave labour.*

I dropped off a little from the Church and was taking more and more part in the City Mission. The months rolled by and Milton's Store got busier and busier. As December approached. And more and more demands were made on me. They also took on a weekend girl so much more up market than me, also light in colour like the Milton's. She had proper lunch breaks and just stood behind the counter looking like part of the furniture, while I run around getting all the jobs done. She was told to go as soon as it was closing time, I had to stay behind, clean up the stores and then cream Mrs Milton's Face and comb her hair. More for comfort than effect!! Christmas Eve night, a night I will never forget, we were so busy. The shop was packed. Even the week end girl worked until 10pm, she was given a Christmas bonus in a pay slip envelope. I worked and how I worked, constantly lifting and carrying, fetching and moving big large clumsy unwieldy items. Demands were made on me to go to this department or to somewhere else in the store. I was rushed off my feet, my back was wet with sweat and I was kept on the go until 1pm in the morning, then had to clean and tidy up the shop while the day's takings were counted. My reward, a Christmas bonus of two shillings and sixpence (today's currency 25p!) was pushed in to my hand. I was dead on my feet, my body ached. My arms felt like lead, I was sweaty, hot and dusty from the long days toil. I was exhausted; my legs were trembling and I was so hurt seeing how badly I was treated. I cried and cried on the way home. I gave Uncle the money and he went mad. He said I should have thrown it in her face; she was using me as 'slave labour'

Christmas passed, but my heart had lost its happiness and I started wondering more and more what was going to happen to me. I did pay a visit to the Church and heard during the announcements that the Cadets (Trainee Officers) were coming to Montego Bay on a ten day 'Alleluia campaign'. I made a few more visits and got caught up in watching these cadets from the big city of Kingston (Jamaica's Capital) when I was on errands to the bank or building society would run to the hall and spend a few moments listening to them. They looked so smart in their white uniforms as they marched from place to place. I started to chat to them and ask how to become a cadet? They were all very friendly. After the ten day campaign was over, my mind started to work overtime again about my future. One day I had a bright idea I went to see the Captain (The Minister) at the Church Hall and asked how could I become a cadet? I also explained about my background and he seemed to understand. He said he would help me as best he can. I also spoke to Eugene the girl who lived with the minister at the City Mission about my problems and how I would like to go to Kingston to be trained as a Missionary. But I needed somewhere to stay. She told me she had an aunty living in Kingston and she would write and ask if she could help me. I had to tell my Uncle That I would like to become a missionary but I needed to live in the big city of Kingston to be near the Church Training College. I also told him the Captain that he would like a word with him. He did go and was satisfied that I would not be wandering about the town and alone. Eugene's Aunty took a long time to reply to her letter. In the mean time I was to be baptised and was looking forward to the important occasion. This took place one cool cloudy Sunday morning. When I was fully immersed in the sea, baptised and became a true follower of God.

# CHAPTER 15

## *Kingston the big city*

I never forgot how badly I was treated that Christmas Eve night by Mrs Milton and I was only a matter of time before I would be off. At last a letter arrived from Eugene's Aunt and everything would be fine. Oh! I could not wait to let the Milton's know that I was leaving. The day came for me to tell her and nothing was going to stop me. That soon pull her up; she wanted to know if I needed more pay, if there was anything she could do for me in any way. Perhaps she could ease some of the duties I did, but it was all too late I was hurt too much and I turned down all her offers. She was almost pleading with me to stay, saying how loyal and trustworthy I was, how I was a very conscience worker and how much they would miss me. She suddenly realised that no longer could they pay a worker such a low wage and get away with it. I was glad that I had made the decision and somehow felt free; I was no longer in chains. I told my friends at the City Mission I would be leaving them and they were very surprised and said they would be sad to see me go. The time came and they held a lovely farewell meeting for me, which was very touching and a memory I have treasured. After the meeting was over, I was thinking, Kingston here I come. Penniless, but I am coming anyway, with God in my heart and very little in my battered suitcase and nothing in my purse!

Now Kingston lay in the shadow of the Blue Mountain Range, and their lofty peaks were generally hidden in the heat haze or white fluffy clouds that surrounded the area. The city was the big exciting place, full of bustle, noise and vibrant colour. There were People, Buses, Taxi's, Cars Horse and cart everywhere. Sophisticated stores and boutiques down every street. And Higglers (Market stall traders)l selling their wares on the pavements. The harbour was full of huge ships bringing tourists or trade to the Island and for a young girl this was an exhilarating and thrilling place to be. My Uncle insisted on coming with me to Kingston, for the city was not without its dangers and we finally found the address where I was to stay. We were made welcome by two elderly couple and a teenager called 'Gerty' She was another victim of the child labour abuse, which was so common in Jamaica in those days. A poor underprivileged youngster from either the country parts, or poor relatives, used to be sent to people who were in a slightly better position than themselves. They were told they were going to have a better life with better opportunities, but ended up as domestic slaves/servants and all that entailed. It brought another pain to my heart the minute I heard the couple speak to Gerty and again I thought of my poor brothers and sister who were in a no doubt similar situation.

I listened to Uncle making the usual promises that he would be sending food and a little money when he could. I was given my instructions and the time came when my Uncle had to say "Goodbye" A new life had started for me with a small meal and a lot of questions asked. I could sense these people had two sides to them. One for me, and the other side for poor Gerty. I was treated with respect while she was treated with contempt and cruelty. I felt sad for the girl, she was almost begging to be praised, rushing around and doing all the chores that were put upon her. I offered to help but each time I was told "That Gerty would do them". I decided to keep quiet and weigh the whole thing up. When it came to our bedtime she was told to get the bedding out, which she quickly did. In no time had made up two beds, one on the couch for me and one on the floor for her in the little sitting room. I whispered to her to have the couch, but she whispered back but she said the lady would be 'Bex' (angry and quarrel) Soon we settle and everywhere was quiet. Except for the constant noise of the dogs barking in the yard, which was another common thing in Jamaica. We used to say 'they are sending messages to one another' The days were going quickly and Thursday came at last, and I told the couple I would be out all evening at the Church. (After all that's was what I was there for} It was a very long walk to the Salvation Memorial Hall situated in North parade which was in down town Kingston.

Four buses past me by and I could see some of the Church people in their white uniforms inside. I could not flag a bus down because the few pence I carried, had to last me for the week. I eventually arrived, Hot tired but glad to be there and see all those people in their uniforms going up the and surprised at the number of white folks who were there as well. As a girl the only white people I saw in Montego

Bay were tourists. The days passed by but I could not find work. I was getting desperate and embarrassed as I wanted to give the couple something for my keeps. One day the lady (whose name has slipped from my memory) sent Gerty and me to step in to the local market hall. I have never seen so many gathered together at the marketplace. Gerty had been given all the instructions and I was there to help and carry. We stopped at a little stall to look at some face cream and were told to try it. Being young girls we giggled and rubbed the cream well in. Well a reaction set in and made my face look as if I was about to have a heart attack. The sweat was pouring off me, and as fast as I was wiping the perspiration away, it came back. It didn't affect Gerty at all. People around were asking if I was unwell? Gerty said she would go and fetch someone and she was a long time coming back (I think she went to see her boyfriend) I was getting worried when she eventually arrive and without an explanation. When we got back to the house I have never seen such cruelty. They treated Gerty worse than a wild animal. They beat her with a strap they punched her shouted and screamed at her and left her sobbing in a corner covered in marks from her beating. I made up my mind I was not going to live under the same roof as these people and again the uneasy thoughts of my brothers and sister were probably being treated in the same way. (I was to find out in later years my feelings were correct. they too suffered dreadfully under brutal unfeeling Guardians)

# Chapter 16

## Mother Sheringham

After a few weeks I went to have a word with the lady who was in charge of the Church Cadets when they came to Montego Bay to ask if she knew anywhere I could stay and nearer to the Church as it was such a long lonely and dangerous walk on my own at nights. She told me she knew of someone and as soon as she can she will have a word with her. I spoke to her again and she told me to go to an address in Allman Town (A district in Kingston) I had to ask for 'Mother Sheringham' She sometimes take girls from the country and look after them until they get work. I was also told she was a wonderful Christian woman. So one day I went to see this lady, a giant of a person who must have been in her seventies. She look me up and down then told me to get my things and come. I did not feel exceptionally happy but at least I would be going to the Army more often and more freely. Mother Sheringham was an 'Old time Salvationist' full of 'Blood and Fire (the Church Motto) and very loud hallelujahs above everyone else. But Mother was not what she seemed to be, and very quickly I was back in the old routine of cooking, scrubbing, cleaning, and doing the general housework chores. I seemed to be a walking disaster, for everywhere I went, life became harder for me. Each morning I was up at 6 am preparing and cooking meals. After prayers there was Mother Sheringham's slop pail daily to empty. I used to feel sick with the smell and the cleaning of the bucket. One small light relief was Mother's parrot (Polly) I have never in my life hear a bird talk so clearly. It could sing, say the Lords Prayer word for word. One song the parrot used to sing which I will always remember was:-

*Lord in thy love and thy power make me strong*
*All that may know that to thee I belong*
*When I am tempted, let this be my song*
*Cleansing for me, cleansing for me*

So 'Thank you Polly' it was a song that kept me going.

There was a girl called Daisy, who used to come over two or three times a week help and line the baskets for Mother Sheringham who sells them to the tourists who comes off the ships in downtown Kingston, Daisy used to come about eight o'clock in the evening, and work right through until three or four in the morning. From time to time she ended up in Kingston General Hospital suffering from asthma which I thought was brought on by over work and exhaustion. Every morning about 9 am, Mother would leave the house and not return until 6pm. She lock everywhere up, except a little side room which was only a passage used as a dining area. And in this passage was a table which doubled up as an Ironing Board and a long narrow bench. Each day I was given my breakfast consisting of a piece of bread and a mug of tea. I was also given my instructions and duties to do. I had to make the dogs porridge of cornmeal with milk water and sugar. I had to clean the passage then sweep the yard; I had to burn wood for charcoal everyday, and I had to do the washing no matter how big or small the bundle was. And it must be done and ironed before Mother Sheringham got back in the evening. I drank a lot of water during the day or take a little of the dogs porridge for I was desperately hungry. Even though I made the porridge and know it was clean, the thought that it was for the dog made me sick. I didn't do this very often because Mother told me where the porridge should reach in the saucepan. When I did take out a little porridge, I had to boil it up again so as not to show the old mark on the inside of the pan. She never leave me any lunch. I got used to being hungry and sometimes lay on the long narrow bench and sleep from hunger tiredness and boredom. I never had any friends except those I meet at church and in the shops. I wasn't allowed to leave the yard during the day. Oh! I was really stupid in those days, and did everything I was told. Never using my own mind and always out to please. When Mother Sherringham arrives in the evening she would feed the dogs, then she would look around to see if I had done all the chores.

When satisfied she would count out the food for me to cook. It didn't matter about me, her meal and for two of her friends who used to come there; they must get a proper serving. If I was to get three pieces of food on my plate I was really lucky and even better if I had a piece of meat or fish. But the hunger was always there I suppose I existed between 200 to 500 calories a day. I was always hoping things would get better for me.

One day a lady who worked for Mother Sherringham's

son came in to the yard. She shouted "Miss May where you are?" I came out of the large woodshed to find out what was it Mrs Davis wanted? She said "I hope you haven't finished your lunch yet because I have come to share with you. This morning I come out of the house in such a temper, I left my lunch box on the table." How could I tell her that I had nothing to give? But she ask again "Can you share yours" I laughed and she ask why am I laughing but I said nothing. She looked at her watch and ask again. I was forced to say "I had no lunch". She gave me a long hard look and said "hasn't Mother left you any"? I had to say it was true. She then said "How long has this been going on" and said "As long as I have been here. To my surprise Miss Davis she started crying and I said it was O.K as I was used to not having anything to eat during the day. Miss Davis called Mother a few not too kind words and said "Stay here I will be back" I thought she had gone to the shop opposite the Post Office but to my surprise she returnedwith Mother Sheringham's door key. We went in the house and she opened the bedroom door and told me to wait outside in case any one comes through the gates. She call me in and said to take a look. I looked inside the trunk at the bottom of the bed and to my shock and disgust, what I thought had contained clothes, was an Ice box containing food and drinks half filling the trunk. Miss Davis took out a bread roll and a slice of fresh ham and gave it to me. At first I said "No" but she insisted. I was frightened and upset and could only nibble at the roll. Miss Davis put everything back, closed the lid then locked the bedroom door, still angry. She said Mother collected the food from the ships when they came in to port and because she was very popular with the lads they bring her gifts and food. Instead of being a good

Christian as everyone thought she was and share it around. She takes it to the White People at Up Park Camp to sell. Now this episode did not stop there Miss Davis said "I had to go home or I will die." She says "It might not affect me now but later on as I get older my body will suffer." I was trapped I did not know what to do?

One day a telegram (No longer used, it was like a text message only on paper) arrived for me. Miss Davis came rushing in to the yard "Miss May, Miss May here is a telegram for you" I opened it up and shouted to her "It's from my Uncle. He said I must go to the railway at a quarter to three and there will be a box of food coming for me" Miss Davis took the telegram look at it then said she was going to change it; here was a chance to get away. She brought it back with words that says "Please come home I am sick" I said "What about the food?" and Miss Davis said "I will have to take it so Mother does not see it" I could see the sense of that, so I agreed. When Mother Sheringham came home that evening I presented her with the Telegram. She looked at me, her eyes narrowing and said "Wen did dis a come? (When did this come?) and I told her. She said "Well iffi mus den yoo a go I will len yoo de money fer de train"

(Well if you must then you must, and I will lend you the money for the train) I stood and looked at her I was not sorry to be going home, she was cruel and unkind. Next day I had to get up even earlier to do all the household duties and chores. The diesel (Train) left for Montego Bay at 3pm but I must get all her work done before she left for the ships. She gave me the fare and a few small things that belonged to me anyway. She brought me nothing in the year I spent with her. She told me I must wear my Church Uniform to travel in.

She gave me no money; by the time I reach Montego Bay at 8 o'clock I was extremely hungry and felt faint. On the train up everyone around me was eating or selling fresh fruit or food. I had no money for anything.

# CHAPTER 17

# More of the same

W hen I came off the train I saw one of Uncles friends who ask me if Mr Kerr knows I was here because he never said 'nuttin' (Nothing) about me coming. I arrived at my gate and the landlady's daughter saw me. She let out a great shout "Cyril! Cyril! Missy Lilly May is ere, wha appen? (Cyril, Miss Lilly May is here, what has happened?) Everyone was gathering around and so I told my story. They were all sorry and sympathetic with me. And then I was given lots and lots to eat and drink. Oh! I felt so much better. But I didn't' last, for soon it was back to the old routine of Cards and Dominoes at my Uncles house. Please God help me to find somewhere nice in Kingston but certainly not to Mother Sheringham that chapter in my life was over.

I wonder what happen to determination these days. I use to hear people say "determination will help you conquer" Well it certainly takes me a long time to conquer? After a few weeks of staying with Uncle, he changed his little house for a slightly bigger one across the yard, and next door to his brother Joseph. It was hardly worth the change, for the boards separating the rooms were so thin. Nothing changes except that I had grown up a bit more and was even prouder than before. I knew the men were tipping their hats to me and bowing even lower. I just wanted to be different. I felt that even without much education one can still be somebody. I never made an attempt to find work because I did not want to work in my home town anymore. The girls I once knew were either at High School, working or having babies. I could not believe so much had happened in such a short time. I kept on at Uncle to write to his brother and wife in Kingston if I could come and live with them? Now Uncles brother (Berty) used to work at the same place as my father in the local Sugar plantation by Barnet Street. Uncle Berty was a Jehovah's Witness and was always pushing his beliefs on my Uncle and trying to convert him when he visited. This made Uncle keep out of the yard for hours and hours. While Uncle Berty ('Bert' for short) hung around for hours and hours for my Uncle to turn up!! Well my determination paid off. I had words from Uncle 'Bert' and his wife, inviting me to stay with them. I was very excited. Once again Uncle took time off and escorted me to the big city of Kingston. On arrival, my Uncle's Brother was waiting for us. He apologised his wife could not come but she was still at work for a big firm that made the most beautiful underwear. Uncle 'Bert' live seven miles from Kingston and it was a lovely three bedroom bungalow set in its own private gardens full of flowers, Bananas, Peas, Yams, Sugar Cane, and there were a few pigs and chickens around as well. I felt so good until Aunty (Who had arrived home by then) started shouting at my Uncle that he should have done something about the child years ago. She didn't know how he could have brought up a child in such awful conditions, with all those men friends around and gambling in the house. I could see that Uncle was looking embarrassed and at that moment I could see life was going to be difficult for Aunty had a sharp tongue. The next morning, breakfast was followed by prayers and I could feel Uncle was glad to be going back home to Montego Bay where he worked. Aunty had a brother (Jason) who was blind and suffered from fits and also living in the house was one of her church sister's daughter, called Caroline. We became good friends. But for me life in that bungalow it was not a happy time, and certainly not a 'Bed of Roses' If you recall, I was a member of the Church and my Uncle and his wife were Jehovah Witnesses. So the pressure on me was terrible. I could not believe after all I had been through with Mother Sheringham I could find one who was a relative be of the same ungodly ways. Although they did things differently, it all boiled down to the same thing, making someone's life so unhappy because they refused to leave one denomination for another. After all we are all serving the same God except we find different ways in expressing ourselves. So were back to old routine of household chores and duties. Caroline and I were up at 6 o'clock each morning and we get Uncle Jason up, help him to the door and to the outside toilet. Sometimes we were faced with some very wet bedding. One of us would change the sheets while the other got on and made the breakfast so Aunty could have hers and then have time to give us our daily duties. A lot of these jobs were repeats. There were days when we did things that were not asked of us, only because we wanted to be loved or praised. But the love or praise never came. The two things we dreaded most. were evenings when Aunty was due home or when a letter arrived from Uncle

'Berty' to say he will be home from Montego Bay (For he worked there too) on such and such a date. Oh! Caroline and I would cringe at the many lies Aunty would tell about us. It was just not fair, for we tried so hard. Caroline was not as soft as me, maybe it was because she did not have the life that I had. The only reason she was staying with Aunty and Uncle because her parents found it too hard to cope with so many children and also her father was ill, so living away meant less strain on the family and one less mouth to feed. One day Aunty decided to travel up to Montego Bay and spend a few days with Uncle 'Berty'. Caroline and I were delighted. Peace at last, if only for a few days.

'No more moaning every evening, and panic every morning. Then Caroline and I had a bright idea. When Aunty had gone, we ask a lady across the road that was quite friendly. If she could look in on Uncle Jason for a while, we told her that we would like to find a job and she was very supportive saying she would see to Jason for us. We set off about a mile in the more up market part of the district knocking on doors asking for work. We had a few funny stares or answers but nothing was available. There was one lady asked me if I washed and ironed my dress. I was surprised at the unusual question but I answered "Yes" What the dear lady did not know, it was my best dress and my white Church Uniform with insignia's (Badges) taken off the collar. I must say it was very white and beautifully ironed. I got the job of looking after her four year old son named Michael. What an over active boy he was and I was warned by his mother do you think you will be able to manage him? I said "I would like to try" I was offered ten shillings a week (Today's money 50p) the only sad thing about the job for me was I ask her if I could live there and she said she wished she had the extra room. Poor Caroline she could not get a job, so we had to make our way home. One of us very happy, and one of us very downhearted. My happiness was short lived, after a few days Caroline said she was leaving. She had got a job through a friend of hers and she will be living in. Miss Babb's the lady across the road said she would continue looking after Uncle Jason, just leave everything in its right place so she could find it.

My job was from 8am till 5.30 pm and I had a long walk each day but I was free. The lady I worked for (Miss Shan) also worked and I had to stay with her son until she arrived back from work. Well one evening I got home to find Aunty in the house. She had come back early only to find out that Caroline had left and I had got a job. She was waiting for me like a 'Fire Eater.' She could not wait for me to get on the veranda. She was terrible and beside herself and her face was red with rage. The whole place could hear her. I was shouted at, and screamed at, that I could just go back and tell the woman I was not coming back and if I didn't then I could pack my case and get out. I was tired and was hungry but no way was she going to let me in, even though it was getting dark outside. And where Miss Shan lived was along a lonely country road but my aunty did not care. "Get back to that woman or get out" she screamed!! But this time she couldn't have cared less. I could have been raped, I could have been attacked, and I could have been robbed or even killed On the days I went to the Church along which was along another road it wasn't so lonely there were more people around But because she hated me so much by going to the Army, she took all her fury out on me and by working at Miss Shan she would lose her unpaid Skivvy and maidservant. Oh I cried so much and had to go back to the lady to tell her I would not be back next day or any other day. She was shocked to see me and thought I had been attacked. If I wanted to defy my Aunty I could stay with a girl who worked for another family. I said "No" because I knew the girl used to have her boyfriend sleeping with her during the day and some nights too. I did not want her to loose her job by telling anyone, so I said I had better go back. Miss Shan she gave me lots of sympathy and a little money and so I walk back along the long road back to my Aunty. She was there with one of her 'Church Sisters' and still full of rage. They were going to Bible Studies and I <u>HAD</u> to go with them. My eyes were swollen from crying and I had nothing to eat and so very hungry and she moaned every step of the way. When we arrived people said I looked sad what was the matter? Before I could get my side of the story, my Aunty launched in to a tirade of how I was being selfish, thoughtless, ungrateful, work shy and uncaring I was, so of course I got the blame for all her shortcomings.

A few months later Caroline came back for a short time. I was delighted as I was lonely and only had one thing to look forward to. Which were the Sunday Meetings and Thursday evening meetings at the Army Hall? I had to ask for sixpence (2½p in today's money) for the return ticket bus fare. Every time there was a lecture. She did not see what I could be gaining from 'that Church' when I could be going the "Kingdom Hall" One Day Aunty came home from work early which did not please Caroline or myself as there was always tension in the house. She never stopped picking about my church or the way Uncle had brought me up with all those men around. I heard it so much I was sick of the moaning and fault-finding. Why was she so bitter? If only I could have worked and earn some money that would enable me to share a room with another girl and help pay the rent! When she arrived home, she opened her bag to reveal some beautiful clothes, shoes and hat all for Caroline. Auntie's church was having a convention the following week. She said "If I wanted clothes like that then I must decide to give up the Church and return to Jehovah". When I refused, she tossed me a piece of grey material and said "You can sew that if you want to go to the convention". I took the fabric and opened it up to find it was already cut in to the shape of a skirt. After she left for work the next day, Caroline and I had a good laugh about it and got the sewing machine out and stitched it up for me. The Saturday afternoon Caroline and I set out for the convention where we would meet up with Aunty. Caroline she looked the perfect picture, in her beautiful outfit. Well as for me, I had my half made skirt. I said half made because it had no zip or poppers only a pin to keep it up. You may think I was tempted to change my church so I could look as good as Caroline but No! I just wanted to belong to the Church. It wasn't long before Caroline left again and I was on my own once more but prayer had been answered. I visited a Chinese Shop across the road and asked if they had any work going. I thought if I mentioned this to my Aunt she would only say "No" But if I got the job, I could look after and see to her brother at the same time. When I asked her, she pulled a face, took a long time to think about it, but in the end grudgingly agreed much to my surprise. I started work on a Monday morning. I already had the experience of serving in Milton's Bookstore so that a big help. There was a very friendly nice young man working there and we got on well together. At first the Chinese couple did not leave me alone and supervised everything I did, but as time went on they started trusting me. I felt good, and no way was I going to let them down. There was only one thing which I disagreed with them was, I was told not to give a full measure of anything. I pleaded with them and told them about my beliefs and the church but they would not back down. Every day I suffered from a guilty conscience with "Thou shalt not steal" was ringing in my heart and my head each time I served a customer. The work was easier than I had ever done before and I was given five shillings (25p in today's money) every week. We used to look forward to closing the shop on a Saturday evening. The young man (I can not remember his name) used to buy a tin of sardines some bread and share it with me. The lady used to stay as well and stock the shelves and we would all share some jokes together. They were good employers, kind and caring. The lad was good fun and friendly and without any strings attached we would say our "Goodnights" and go our own way. I only had to run across the road and give Aunty my pay packet.

She still only gave me sixpence (2½p) for my bus fare and a penny for the church collection, which I now felt brave enough to ask for. She never gave me any money out of my wages, a new dress or extras. Everything I had was old but kept clean and smart. I was working but getting nothing out of it. It just did not make sense and I was still no way forward. One evening I asked Aunty if I could visit a friend at the School for the Blind, At Slipe Pen Road in lower Kingston. She gave me a disapproving stare but agreed I could go. I then ask for some bus fare please which she reluctantly gave me. Before the job at the Chinese Store I would never have asked for fare other than the church, but I felt I had worked for it and was contributing to the household budget. I caught the bus and went to the School to see my blind friend. A delightful girl whom I normally spoke to on a Thursday night, She was so pleased to see me and took me to meet some of the other girls who were also blind. While I was there I ask to see the lieutenant whom I knew from Montego Bay when she was a cadet. I opened up my heart to her telling her of my problems. I told her if I wasn't getting to the Army then I wouldn't let it bother me. But I might end up in my Auntie's church just to keep the peace. She mentioned that her Mum and Dad (Church Captains) were looking for a nice girl to help them. They were not her real parents but she used to spend a lot of time at their house when they were stationed in her home town in Panama, She said her own mother used to drink a lot, so she turned to this couple who showed her a lot of love. And they were very popular with the young people too. I was getting excited at the thought life was going to change for me again. (Please God let it be better I prayed) The Lieutenant arranged for me to meet her Mum and Dad who seemed very nice but from my previous experiences I withheld my judgement. They told me they really needed someone to be on hand because Captain (the man) had a very bad heart problem and had to take life a little easier. Mrs (Captain) had to do a lot of visiting as part of her ministry and missionary work. If I was at the house I could help with the chores and running errands, and it would give her a chance to get on better without worrying about her husband. Well that was sorted out and it was time to tell my aunt I had the offer to stay with a Church family. I also tried to point out in a gentle way that I would not have the long walk home when I got off the bus at nights. As I expected, she nearly burst a blood vessel at the news and so shocked, she thought she had me at her place for life. She wanted to know how long this had been going on, and what about my job at the shop? Why was I doing this? I wanted to tell her that I was working to better myself and not be a slave for her. But I kept my peace, for in those days you were told you never too big to be hit. (Manners were the order of the day, especially to your elders) Aunty was really angry and went on and on. Uncle 'Berty' came down from Montego Bay and of course that was topic of the week. How lazy I was, how ungrateful I have been.

# CHAPTER 18

## *On the move again*

I worked my notice at the Chinese Shop, got my clothes in the best order possible and I had hoped Aunty would give me some money but no such luck, none was forthcoming (I suppose I should have realised that). Uncle 'Berty' offered to take me to the city to meet the Captains. They met he handed me over and then left. Mrs Captain had to go somewhere so (Mr) Captain took me home to their Quarters (As they are called). My heart lifted the minute I got to the gates. There was a lovely Church hall just inside the yard and next door was the Captains House. It was well laid out and I even had my own room complete with single bed, chair, dressing table and wardrobe to hang my clothes. I was glad when Mrs Captain came back so she could tell me what my duties would be. We had lunch and they talked about what help that would be needed. I suppose I would be about sixteen years old then but I seem to have done a whole life time of going around in circles, and getting nowhere. I did so hope this new life was going to be better. My spirits were lifted and I felt so much happier. I was better fed, I had my own room. I could attend The Army meetings every Thursday and Sunday. I was treated more like a daughter than a work horse. Although I did have to work hard, there was not the fault finding and criticisms which my Aunty used to carry on with. The Captain got out of breath quite a lot and I was worried a few times about him. Mrs Captain told me to call her 'Mum' and Captain 'Dad' as the other young people in Panama used to call them. It sounded very strange to say it, as we were always brought up to say "Yes Aunty" or "Yes Uncle" and NEVER their Christian name!! Only if you wanted a 'Fat Lip'!! (As they say in Jamaica!) She was a very kind and caring lady but the Captain was very moody which I put down to his health problems. And after a while the Captain was finding every thing I did was wrong. And so my feeling of contentment and well being, slowly slipped away, and I was back to thinking, It was all too good to be true. Was I ever going to find happiness? Now the Church uniforms in the West Indies are made of white gabardine, so Mum used to send Dads own to the laundry while I washed and ironed hers and mine along with all the other clothes and sheets. In those days there were no washing machines and the iron was the old flat iron that used to be heated up on a little charcoal fire. It meant constant wiping off the charcoal from the bottom of the iron but that's how it was done. This load of washing and ironing reminded me of the children who had to do all the work before school and finish off when they came back. I didn't have to attend school so the captain kept me working nonstop giving me job after job. I had to be up early in the morning to get myself ready and then start the breakfast. There was always egg, toast marmalade, marmite and cheese. Now dad had to have his egg hard on the outside and the yoke had to be 'waxy' in the middle or there would be trouble! ...... There were troubles most mornings! As I could hardly get the egg to his requirements, and had to put up with his constant nagging about how it should be done. I use to ask Mum if she would do it for me but she couldn't get it right either. It was then I discovered it wasn't the egg that was his problem, it was 'Me'. Mum started giving me money to buy the groceries from a shop across the road. It was some Chinese friends of theirs. She also gave me some good advice about cooking and some of the recipes I still use today. She never cook herself but told me in a nice way, how she wanted it to be done. On many occasions she told me not to take any notice of what Dad says. I could not stand the way he spoke to me like I was a paid servant. I never was paid! But I stayed, for I had good food, a good bed and an easy access to the Church Hall. If only he meant it when he prayed so fervently but it was for other people not me.

CHAPTER 19

# *A Cuban comes a callin'*

I just didn't know why people treated me the way they did? I was not rude, I did not steal, I did not answer back I tried to please. I had a pleasant nature. And I was always clean and tidy. (My Uncle was very strict on my appearance) Maybe there was something wrong with me I wasn't aware of? Dad kept on at me so much I find life was back to where it all started when I was much younger. One Thursday evening I was ironing Dads uniform. Oh I dreaded doing his clothes, anyone who washed, starched and ironed a white uniform jacket and trousers can tell you it is not easy. Especially for a sixteen year old who had never had to do it before. If there was a slightest mark on any of these garments, then they had to go back in to the wash again. Remember I am using a flat iron heated by charcoal and wash by hand all week to keep it down. Washing starts on Mondays and finishes Thursday mornings. That's the big wash, Sheets. Underlay's, Table cloths and sometimes curtains. Uniforms were to be ready for the big evening meetings, Ironed starched and pristine white. More and more Dad seems to dislike me and I tried so hard to please him. One day Mum told me they were going to the country with some relatives for a day out by the sea. I was hoping with all my heart they would take me with them.

Two days before they were due to go, they told me who was going and would I get some chicken and make a packed lunch. They must have seen the disappointment on my face because straight away Dad said "You won't be on your own I have asked someone to come round and do the garden". In the same breath he said "And I want no rude behaviour" I was shocked; No one ever hinted such a thing to me before, I had never given any cause for flirting or even dating. I did not answer; I turned away with tears filling my eyes. When he had gone, Mum came and put her arm around me and said "Don't worry I trust you" The day came for Mum and Dad to leave. The relatives arrived and collected them. Peace at last! I quickly did all my work as I was instructed. And everything looked lovely. The floors were shining like mirrors, Peas was in soak for Sunday dinner and the meat was marinated. I dusted and tidied the Army Hall which previously had a big clean during the week with the help of some members. I did all my chores so I could have the afternoon to myself to rest and read as I never get much chance. Promptly at 12 o'clock the gardener arrived. His name was Donald a nice young man who like me had very sincere feelings about the Lord. He was kind and helpful when asked to do something. Donald and I would share a joke and laugh from time to time. I soon found out Dad did not like this, and so when he was around, I was a little cool and withdrawn towards the poor chap. around 10.30 pm a car pull up at the gate. Donald I was sitting on the front veranda, me in one chair and he in another. No sooner had Mum and Dad and his niece got out of the car, Dad shouted us "What are you still doing here at this time of night and what have you been getting up to"? Oh the shock of it, I was seething with anger. I could hear Mums voice saying "What's got in to you? They are only waiting up for us" Donald was very upset and said "What do you think we are doing Captain? We were sitting here worried and hoping you get home safely and all the time you are thinking nasty thoughts. He made it quite clear he was not going to come back and stormed off. If we were sitting close together I could understand his outburst. In those days (Late 1950's) youngster wouldn't be seen holding hands or showing any display of affection in public. I stopped talking to Dad. I had to keep quiet or I would say something that would send me packing. I even went on a mini hunger strike by eating very little and only spoke at the table when Mum spoke to me. I know I was only hurting myself but it would let Dad know he can't go around making insinuations. It took a lot of coaxing and begging for Donald to come back to Rae Town Corps. That was where the Church Hall was, and also the Captains Quarters. Everything was happening! I met a really good looking Cuban boy as I was collecting money for the Army and selling 'War Cry's' (The Church Newspaper) Each Friday Mum, Vincent (Another young man from the Army Corps)) would go down to Kingston Harbour (The Water Front) as we called it then, and occasionally I was asked to accompany Mum when Vincent couldn't be there. One particular day Mum could not make the time to go, she ask if I would accompany Vincent. I was not particularly pleased as I already had a run in with Dad about Donald. Anyway I had no choice so off I went. This Cuban took a shine to me and went back on his ship The *SS Evangeline*, to get me a present

I said "No" only because I was worried what Dad would say. Vincent told me to take the parcel. He also told me that every week Mum gets things given to her from the cabin crews or dock workers. Sometimes she showed me, other times she didn't; occasionally she gave me a bar of soap. 'Mother Sheringham' I thought. Sounds like history repeating itself.

I was given a large margarine tin (No plastic in those days) and also a parcel of ham and bread rolls. Oh! I could not wait to show Mum and to share it with her. We left the 'Water Front' about 5.30pm. We also felt good because we had made a lot of money for all the social work and care the Church did around the town. When I opened the tin there were soaps of all different colours with lovely scents.

These I shared with Mum. The food was delicious, I had never tasted meat so beautiful, and it melts in your mouth. We shared the rolls and ham with a couple of elderly ladies who Mum knew. They were thrilled. Dad actually made a nice comment about our collecting. I must have done something right at last because I was sent out more often and I was getting used to going. The ship which the Cuban boy was on came to Kingston every fortnight and the lad came out to see me and brought me presents. This time my mind was telling me to be more careful. He not only want to give me presents but to take me out. I said "No thank you" I told him I would not be allowed to. He got friendly with Vincent because he could speak a little Spanish and could tell me what he was saying. Vincent told me he wanted to come and see the Captains. Oh No! Panic set in and even more panic when I got home. Vincent had told Mum and Dad what the Cuban lad had said, and Dads face looked like thunder. It was even worse when I opened the parcel for there inside, were two pair's of knickers and soaps. He told Vincent to tell me, he had brought some shoes or slippers but was not allowed to take them off the ship. I quickly told Mum to take whatever colour knickers she wanted. They could not fit her of course because she was quite a big woman. She never shared the one she got because she always say "They are for her Nieces" Anyway she took one and some soap. Two weeks later the *SS Evangeline returned* to Kingston and we were selling 'War Cries' (The Church Newspaper)at the water front the lad came to speak to Vincent telling him 'He want to marry me' and will be coming home with us. I pleaded with both of them but they acted as if it was nothing to do with me. I was almost running behind them begging for them to stop. Dad would be sending me back to Mo' Bay. Oh I was so upset. We arrived home and Vincent told Dad why the lad was there. Both Mum and Dad spoke Spanish and telling me everything. I said "I did not bring him here, and I did not want to get married either" After some refreshments the Cuban lad and Vincent left. My heart was beating fast because I knew it wasn't finished yet. Dad waited for me to make tea and then the lecturing started. I said a few simple things in my defence but he wasn't listening and he went on and on. It was no better when a letter arrived from Cuba. I took it straight to Mum She went in to the bedroom where Dad was, I followed her in. She told Dad about the letter and of course he glared at me. Mum translated the letter out to me as it was in Spanish. I had been invited to Cuba to meet the boy's parents, his five sisters and his brother. I made it quite clear that I didn't want to go and meet anyone or go to Cuba and asked Mum if she could dictate a letter to that effect and send it off straight away.

Dad called me; he wanted to have a quiet word.

# CHAPTER 20

# Attempted Rape

Oh No! They are going to send me home through no fault of my own, I thought. Any way, it wasn't that, Dad was asking me (even in a fatherly way,) not to think about going out with this boy because they can treat their wives very badly. I again said that I was not going to marry anyone and I had no wish to go to Cuba. I also said I didn't know the lad that well. And with that he seemed satisfied and relieved. Since the incident with Donald on the veranda it was the first time he tried to be nice to me. Maybe Mum told him to be a bit kinder or I might just pack up and go. And the letter Mum sent off to the lad did not seem to work either, because one night Mum's relative came to see Dad who wasn't very well. We were all on the veranda talking, when we heard the gate. We looked up to see the Cuban boy. I panicked and said to her come with me, I shouted at the lad "You are not allowed to come here. Go away". The poor chap looked shocked and disappointed; he rushed off never to be seen again. I must admit I felt awful at shouting at him for he had never done me any harm. Mums relative wanted to know what that was all about saying how wonderful and handsome he looked. I was then told off for not even showing hospitality when he came all that way from the Water front. I just didn't seem to do right for doing wrong, but I was terrified that Dad would start all over again.

I have from time to time wondered how he was, and must have settled and now had his own family. Well as I said before, Dad started to get quite friendly, but on hindsight and what happened I know the reason why. I was young and naïve at the time and was told by friends and grown up's how pretty I looked, but of course you think they were being nice and you never really believed them.

One Day Mum was out doing her visits when Dad came to my room to have a rest. He always said my room was the coolest. This particular day I was trying to do so much in one go. I was cooking a lovely dish of stew peas and rice as well as polishing the floors. I was always working to be praised and to please but it didn't always work. I finished the cooking, laid the table and made some cool lemonade with fresh limes in as I waited for Mum to return. I started mopping the polished floors working my way through the house to my room. I was just about to pass Dad lying quietly on my bed, I thought he was asleep, when his foot caught me like a big hook and pulled me off balance on to the bed. Before I knew what was I was happening, he was on top of me. Down went the mop with a clatter. I fought him as hard as I could shouting "No! No! get off me" His hands got in to my pants and all I could think of is 'I hope he has a heart attack' He put one hand across my upper chest whilst his big body pinned me down, and tried to undo his zip with the other. I struggled with him screaming and shouting with all the strength I had. He rolled off, gasping and panting like he really wants to die. I ran out of the room. As I ran past the window in the dining room, I caught a glimpse of a white uniform. I dashed in to the kitchen to tidy myself up and pretended to stir the pot. Footsteps came on to the veranda, it was Mum. "Hello" she said, where is 'Manny'? As she called him, I did not answer; maybe she thought I did not hear her. I had no idea what Dad was doing? Mum was in her room maybe getting changed as she knows if he wasn't in his room at that time of the day, he would be in mine. That wasn't unusual, I brought in the dinner, my hands shaking and feeling a little weak at the knees. Dinner was strange for me. Dad he jus' talk and talk non stop. Wanting to know everything Mum did while she was out. I just let him get on with it while I think and eat slowly. I could not make up my mind what to do? The rest of the day went off without troubles.

I was glad to get to bed so I could lay there and work my problems out. If I was to tell anyone they would not believe me. He was such a well loved man and well respected by young and old alike. I tried to work out all the months I had been there maybe I did something to cause it? No, as far as I knew I never showed any interest in him only as a father. I decided to let the matter rest but the incident kept popping back in to my head. How I was nearly raped by the man I trusted and called Dad and was also my Minister. There was definitely some jinx on me for as I grew older things got worst, what was I going to do with my life?

You are not going to believe what happened next! A few weeks passed when Mum told me Dad had to have an assistant to help with the church work as he was getting worst. Church Headquarters sent them a letter confirming this and it was to be a lieutenant. (A Junior Minister) I ask if I had to leave. Mum said she did not want me to go was I was a great help, not only in the house and Sunday school I was a good all rounder. She said I could share her bed, if the lieutenant was nice, later she would ask if I could move in to her room. Well I had more troubles and worries to pray about. The list gets longer each day. A few months later the Lieutenant arrive, and she seemed a pleasant person. Dad still never showed or let me know how sorry he was for doing what he did. I could never listen to him preach again as I thought over and over again what he had tried to do. How could he stand there and tell people to be better Christians. While all the time he himself was so deep in sin?

Well life was getting on and I shared Mums big bed with her. I made sure I changed in the sitting room or in the bathroom outside. I did not like the arrangements because Mum had no privacy, it wasn't right. But Mum said she did not mind. I still felt bad about it. My mind was working overtime and I thought he will attack me again because he cannot sleep with his wife. One day I put this to the Lieutenant saying Mr Captain did not get a chance to be with his wife as I was sharing their bed. She said it was O K to come and stay her room it was not a problem. And so I moved in. A few weeks later she was out visiting her friends and she came back late. I was sleeping she woke me up and ask if I was OK and started telling me of her evening. Then without any warnings she said "You have never given me a good night kiss" I said "Oh sorry, you see Mum gets a kiss at nights" so that was no big deal. Then she moved over and started to touch my private parts. I was shocked rigid. I then jumped up and shouted at her "Wha you tink yu adoo"? (What did she think she was doing?) I heard footsteps, it was mum asking if everything alright. I could not answer I was shaking with anger. The lieutenant shouted back "Lilly May was dreamin" I still said nothing and Mum went back to her own room. Anyway I was not dreaming because she was found out a couple of years later she was a lesbian and was asked to leave. I felt trapped, after the incident with Dad, and now the Lieutenant I felt so alone, ashamed and frightened. I was a walking disaster to myself. What was I going to do?

# CHAPTER 21

## *A new start. A new job*

After the night of the second shock, I decided to try and find work somewhere else. I had another great idea. They always seem great when they are thought over, and you are alone with your feelings. Maybe one works out everything the way you would like it to be. But life is never like that, Life is not a dream, it is real One Thursday evening, after the meeting I went over to speak to some of the children from the School for the Blind, and hopefully to have a word with Captain Wicks. the manager in charge, I managed to get my request in about a job at the School and he said he "Would look in to it" for me! I told Mum when I arrived home and she hoped something would turn up for me. A few weeks passed and I felt I must ask the Captain again if anything had come up? He told me they were starting a new project and would let me know the following week. Oh! How the days dragged by; Friday slowly came and slowly went. Saturday was slower still. Sunday always a busy day so that wasn't too bad. Monday another slow slow day Tuesday and Wednesday was the same. 'THURSDAY' At last it I was

Thursday and I would know if I had a job there. Please, Oh Please God help me. I prayed so hard as I have done over the years. The Evening Meeting came. I hardly took it in, as I was so anxious to speak to Captain Wicks and then the meeting was over. I rushed across the hall to speak to him and he said "Yes come up to the School and see my wife" Oh! Thank you Lord, perhaps my time of trial is over? So on the 17th Of September I walked in to the School full of hope for the future. If I get the job whatever it is I will still be able to go to church. It would be close at hand and I could even walk there. I was called in to the office and there sitting at a desk in front of me, was a small white lady Mrs Captain Wicks in a very crisp and starched Army uniform who had a kind and trusting face and she seemed to look right in to my soul as she listened to my story and why I need the job right away. She was very sympathetic and said if I was willing to share with some of the senior ladies until they could fix up a room for me, then I could start next week. You can imagine the happiness I felt as I went home. Perhaps this time it would be better. Perhaps this time I would really find contentment, perhaps this time I would not be treated as a workhorse!

All these thoughts were tumbling through my head. On reaching the house I rushed in and told Mum the good news and she was very please for me and said I could come back and visit them any time. Mum was fine, always kind to me but Captain and the Lieutenant. Well I just did not want to see them again. And so the day came and I set off to my new job and to my new way of life to new surroundings, and new people to meet and get used to. When I arrived at the School, by the way, (the Schools proper name was) 'The Church School for the Blind and Visually Handicapped Children'

Shortened locally to 'The School for the blind' I headed for the office to see my new boss Mrs Captain Wicks. I was given a warm welcome and introduced to the captain I would be working under, a pleasant lady from Antigua. And I should see her if there were any problems. I was told what my work involved and then taken on a tour of the school, after which I was taken to my room inside the ladies dormitory which I would share with another person and would be a temporary measure. I found the senior ladies and older girls were quite good fun and we had lots of laughs and I tried to be helpful as I could with the little experience I gained working with my auntie's blind brother Uncle Jason. There was a carpenter at the School by the name of Mr Jones who came to me and said "The Captain told him to build a room inside the small girls dormitory" I was thrilled, even though I would miss out all those laughter's we had in the mornings and again when they returned in the evenings. Every day They used to travel to the Workshops for the Blind at Allman Town. (Another part of Kingston) The day came when Mr Jones had finished my lovely little room. Captain Wicks asked me where I would like my new furniture Oh I loved it. Also in the room, was a louver window where I could keep an eye on the girls in the dormitory? My official title was 'Housemother' and I was the first Housemother to be employed at the School. Work started at 6 am. So I was up at 5.30 am to sort myself out before I woke up my new daughters (As I called them) there were seven of them I loved dressing them and doing their hair after all. I had enough experience with Blossom (The landlady's granddaughter in Mo'Bay) West Indian hair is never easy to comb and it was a work of art to keep it neat and tidy. I got them in to a good routine.

Off with all the bedclothes, folded, and put on to a chair or stool. Beds had to be stripped. Mattresses were turned and the girls sent off to the bathroom to get washed and teeth brushed. On their return they had to make up their bed by feeling the hem of the sheet or blanket and knowing which side was top or bottom. My help was always needed and I felt like real mum. I was told that an officer would come and help with the girls, but usually she come when all the work was done. So I had to use a lot of 'Common Sense' and pride myself that I still use to-day which goes a long way to make up for my lack of good education. There was a little girl called Pearl who followed me around and she had quite a lot of sight. She was always willing and helpful. Although only seven I could count on her for help and information. It did not take me long to have everything down to a fine art.

The children also had other duties to perform like getting their classrooms dusted. Help to lay the tables in the dining room, helping with the washing up, and always with the aid and guidance from the staff or even older girls. I was fascinated how these girls and boys, some completely blind others partially sighted could be so clever. Some I found out came from very poor backgrounds. As time went on, me discover the youngsters had even greater talents. They could play the piano; sing, type letters and read books using the Braille method and could read even better than I could. I took a lot of pride in my work, I enjoyed walking in to the dormitory and looked at the floors which was always lovely and shine. The school worked on a bell system and the first bell in the morning was to tell us to get a move on as it would be nearly time for breakfast. The second bell we would set off set off for the dining room. We would assist the children at the tables and when they had finished, and cleared away, the staff would, have their breakfast while the children went back to brush their teeth again and get ready for assembly and school. I always tried to get back to the dormitory to make sure all my girls were well turned out. Mrs Captain Wicks also checked the children as they went up the steps to the assembly hall. She had very sharp eyes and missed nothing. If a thing wasn't correct, you would pray for extra blessings to withstand the very firm ticking off by the Captain. As time went on, another House mother was employed this time on the boy's side she was a kind lady and had a motherly figure. The School was growing and there were now over eighty children to see to. Before they brought in more staff, at the age of seventeen I was running two dormitories. The Senior Girls and the younger girls, I was working at full stretch and there were days when I felt so tired but never once complained. I was getting ten shillings a week (50p) and was very grateful. By now I had a couple of new Army uniforms (top priority for me) new shoes and a bag. 'God be praised' I even got some materiel and ask the School dressmaker Mrs James to sew a dress for me. The following week it was paid for and that what I did for a while. I had a few nice dresses and new uniforms hats and shoes. Life had certainly changed, and the very first time in my life 'Happy Birthday' was sung for me on the occasion of my eighteenth birthday and I was given a little gift. It was my first birthday present, something that had never happened before. I was often ask out by the staffs but never took up the offer. I didn't feel the need to go to parties or make up a foursome. I enjoyed my evenings going to meetings, Corps Cadet Gatherings, Young peoples Bible studies or even other church services. When I was not doing that, I would be at the front part of the school where there was a low stage and on there with the senior children learn a new dance or just have fun.

CHAPTER 22

# 'Sticks and Stones again'

Occasionally the staffs would have an evening when they they would ask if you would like to join in, where everyone gets some food, and do a 'Cook Up' as we would call it, They were good and enjoyable times. All that started to change for me when more staffs were employed on the domestic side. There was one woman in particular called Miss Peel. She was a cook, a big woman with an even bigger chip on her shoulder, and supposed to be a Christian at the Adventist Church. 'A very bitter woman indeed' She had two daughters. One a trainee teacher and the other got pregnant, and as far as we all knew was never spoken of as anything worthwhile. While the trainee teacher, her ears must have burned as Miss Peel was crowing about how good her daughter was and what a clever and wonderful teacher she had become. The poor girl was always embarrassed whenever she came to the school because of her mother's constant over the top acclamation of her 'delightful intelligent and charming daughter'. She was a nice girl and always wanted to get away quickly from her mothers constant praise. Miss

Peel didn't like it when the Staffs spoke to the girl, because in her eyes we were far below her daughter's status. She would pass the most unkind remarks each time I went to the kitchen, even though I had never caused her or done her the slightest harm. I could only think it was because I was the only Salvationist among the four House Mother's. I say this, because sometimes I was asked to accompany the children to different functions because they could not spare an officer and I wore the Church Uniform. But in fairness, other House Mothers were also asked. She would shout out "Why was I being favoured I must be the Officer's pet? And saying things like "be careful of Lilly May for she will take your name to the captains at the office and get them dismissed" I was really upset as I would never do anything like that. But you know that 'Mud Sticks' and the staffs would all stop talking the minute I came in to the Dining Room Hall or Kitchen. They would start singing or laughing or make funny remarks and for the first time in a year my life was made hell and I was back to the days of misery and despair. I started going next door to a little Night Class in the School buildings and I felt that I was doing well. The teacher was even encouraging me to work for my Jamaican Locals (Exams equivalent to current GCSE's) I didn't think I had it in me but he obviously thought so. To my surprised the news got around, and two of the staffs who I was told could not read turn up. Now they were some of those who made fun of me for what Miss Peel had been saying. Even though, there was no truth in what the woman had been telling them. It got worse as some of them started to make up lies and going to the office to tell Mrs Captain Wicks about something I did or something I said. A few times I was summoned to the office; my heart was beating as it was going to explode. What am I supposed to have done or said? Now Mrs Wicks was no fool but they were so convincing. I don't think she knew at times what to make of it all. My world was about to close in on me after I had been so happy. One day one of my girls came to tell me they were talking about me in the kitchen and said I was too friendly with the officers and students and they were asking if I was a virgin? I went absolutely mad, and was ready to storm up to the kitchen. I'd had enough. She beg me not to go up there or they would know it was her who told me. My heart was broken to know things had gone so far. So that's why they wanted me to go out with them at nights, to get a man. And they thinks because I wont go with them I am stuck up. The girl said "You know they are working on you for you to leave don't you?

"I know all about that" I said "Only because I am friendly with the officers." I have no guilty conscience, as I have never said or done anything to cause them problem. They are just stupid. No one has accused them of anything yet they are always on the offensive, but why me? I sometimes felt my Christian Faith was being tested beyond endurance. It is amazing; there is a song/hymn in the Church song book that says

> *He gives us more grace as our burdens grow greater*
> *He sends us more strength as our labours increase*
> *To added afflictions he addeth more mercy*
> *To multiply trials he multiplies peace*

Well God saw my deepest needs, and he sent me a friend. One evening a lady called Miss Sewell came to the little night school where I was, not to see me, but to help the teacher who was far from well. I like her straight away and after the class was over we walk to the bus stop which was just outside the School. She was a good Christian lady, and for the first time in a very long while, I felt I was able to open up to someone who had no connection with the Church and could give me some independent advice. It is good to know we are still friends and keep in touch all these years later. Miss Sewell had a gentleman friend who would sometimes call for me on his way up to her. The three of us would call in at different places like the Mineral Baths along the Rockfort Road, which is the West side of Kingston. Or to a drive in meal, (Very popular then) You sat in your car, they hooked up trays to the side and you gave your order and you had your meal sometimes watching a film on the big out door screens.) Or we would take the occasional drive out in to the country for a picnic or to view some scenic part of the local area, they were happy times.

The next day there would be the usual inquisition. Where did you go? Who is the man in the big car? What did you do? What time did you get back? All the time Miss Peel was stirring up the trouble in the background. When I did not answer, then I was guilty of something and they would say I call myself a 'Christian' I only wish I could have had some kindness shown to me by the rest of the staffs, what a relief that would be.

Now one day, an Officer was planted in the store room which was next to the kitchen, The Staff and this Officer were in friendship together. She was from one of the smaller islands in the Caribbean and had a slightly different outlook to those from our own island. The staffs were waiting for me and started on me once again saying I was a sneak, couldn't be trusted, I told tales and all sorts of hurtful things. Of course I defended myself by answering back, and voices got louder and louder. Then the officer burst out of the store room telling me to be quiet because I had been the cause of trouble with the staffs and the cooks. I was livid, I was so angry and gave her a piece of my mind, I then realised that is what the staff had planned, and started the fight to get rid of me. The rule was 'If you are rude to an officer it is 'Instant Dismissal' she ordered me to get to the office at once. I refused, so she stormed off to complain to Mrs Wicks, who in turn sent for me. Still very angry and upset, I went to my room packed my case, and stripped my bed. As I took my bedding to the laundry, I could hear them as I passed the kitchen laughing "Laud we a' dun it, we a' dun it, she a' gan" (Lord we have done it she will have to go now) another one said "oono get rid a' her" (So you have all got rid of her?) I finally arrived at the office to get my 'Marching Orders'. Mrs Wick was working away at her typewriter (A forerunner of the Word processor or Computer) She asked Cynthia (her secretary) to leave the office while she had a word with me. Thank God Mrs Wicks was a fair person. She told me she had listened to the officer's complaint now she wanted to hear my side of the story. She also reminded me of the rules about being rude to an officer. I told her I was guilty of what she had heard and why I had to say it. I could see how she was surprised of what the officer did, and at that moment the School Bell rang and she had to go. She asked me to wait down in my room and she would see me later. I reminded her the Diesel (train) leaves for 'Mo Bay' at 3pm. She ask "Am I just going to walk out on my children like that?" With that comment I felt just a little hope in my heart. I went to my room and put the finishing touches to things like dusting and to the children's cupboard's to tidy their clothes. I thought I would keep the Staffs guessing, and went to sit on the veranda where they could notice me as they served up the children's lunch. The Children came to see me and ask if I was OK. And I said "I might be leaving and I am just waiting for Mrs Wicks to see me" They were crying and begged me not to go. I told them" There was nothing I could do I just had to wait, but don't worry I hope to be there when they had finished school". The afternoon seemed a long way away. I saw the officers come to lunch and I watched them go. It won't be long now I thought before I know what is in store for me. Well here we go, The Boss (Mrs Wicks) will be here in a few minutes and I shall know one way or the other? Now she was a very kind and caring person not just because she took time to listen to my side of the problem. She knew she was not getting the whole truth from the rest of the Staffs. She finally arrive and said "She had thought long and hard about the incident and said there were faults on both sides and tempers had got a little overheated. And in the interest and well being of the children I was still their 'House Mother'"

The dear sweet and very wise Mrs Captain had given me another chance. When my children came to the dormitory that afternoon, I was there to greet them and ask how they got on at school. Of course they were delighted and jumped up and down with happiness that I was not leaving them after all.

Following that episode thing's calmed down a little, but I still had to be very careful and I felt I could not relax, especially in the presence of the staffs when they were around.

A new girl came to work in the Junior Boys dormitory. She was very pleasant and wanted us to have our meals together in the dining room which was a help, because before that, I was eating on my own and there was less chance of Miss Peel or one of her followers putting something in my food to make me ill. Such was the bitterness of that woman.

The School term came to an end and I was asked if I could escort the children home for their main summer holiday, if I took my holiday at the same time. The train makes its way north up to Montego Bay stopping at all the little stations on the way, and there would be quite a few who I could help on to the platforms. Also the parents would be at the stations to collect their children. They ask me to wear my Church uniform So as to be recognised, this of course played right in to the hands of the staffs who had more sneering remarks to give. But I played it 'low key' right up to the day we were to leave. We were given packed lunches and left for the station. All the children were excited at the thought of going home, for no matter how poor some of the homes were, it was still home for them. I saw the last child off at Mo'Bay and I too had someone who really loved and cares about me to meet me at the station. There was my Uncle who looked as if he was off to a wedding, dressed up especially for me. We walked home with me getting the latest news about the family.

I spent a few days with Uncle before he took me to Hanover which was about fifty miles away to spend time with some friends. While I was there I was introduced to a lovely young teacher and I found myself spending more and more time with him and his mother, who was a dress maker. He was very shy, but I could see his mother was

Encouraging him to go out with me. She also said I was the sort of person she would like for her daughter in law. They also owned lots of land, were well respected and rich. Eventually the time came for me to go back to 'Mo Bay'. I was pleased, for I saw him as a good friend but nothing more, I said my 'Goodbyes' to them all. I arrived home and after a few days an old friend of the family who owned a shop across the road and where we did most of the family business. He came to see me. His daughter and I went to school together. I was told his wife had an 'affair' while he was in America and became pregnant. She tried to get rid of the baby and in doing so killed herself. This man kept on calling at our house while Uncle was still at work which made me feel uncomfortable. Then he started to have quiet talks with my Uncle. Two days before I went back to Kingston to start the next school term. I was confronted by this friend and ask for my hand in marriage!! I was shocked and told him I would see him the next day after having spoken to my Uncle. Only to be told that uncle was saying to him for most of the holiday, that he really should have been talking to me. My Uncle for reasons only he knew, did not mention a word to me. Well the next day I kept my promise and said I would write to him when I had settled back in to the School routine. I knew I would not be writing but could not bring myself to hurt anyone by telling them they are not the person for me or I want for myself. He pleaded with me and told me he could buy a large piece of land that was offered to him. It was fully cultivated with citrus trees and that could be my engagement present. I could even sign for it before I went back to Kingston. Another offer was, he could send me to England and then come over and marry me

## CHAPTER 24

## *Fate steps in.*

(As he put it) to save publicity. I was never tempted once, and left for Kingston on August 13th which is unlucky for some, but <u>NOT</u> for me (As you will later find out)

On arriving back at the School, I was asked by a young Scots girl to attend a 'Youth for Christ' meeting with her. I quickly agreed because it was going to be a long quiet evening as the children had not arrived back from their holiday.

I did not know when I left Mo' Bay on the 7.30 a.m Diesel, (Train) my future and whole life would change forever. One of the Officers who were on duty that evening asked if I knew one of David's friends was helping to paint and decorate the boy's dormitory. Now David was an English soldier from Up Park Camp and also a Salvationist who came to help with the Cubs and Boy Scouts at the School. He had be coming for some time, and I knew he was keen on me but I kept giving him excuses or the 'Brush Off' when he would ask me out for a date. I am sad to say I was quite rude to David at times. I, of course knew nothing about his friend, and the officer invited me to walk with her while she put the lights on around the

School which was a normal routine duty when it was getting dark. I went part way and was told to carry on while she went off to the other dormitories. Reluctantly I walked the last few steps to the building where the young soldier was busy painting the walls. I silently peeped in to see the work that had been done, then on 'tip toes' tried to make my way backwards down the steps and back on to the path. I heard a voice from within calling "Hello is someone there? Please come on in" I was a little annoyed to be ask back, as I wanted to get on my way to meet my friend for the Youth For Christ Meeting. Anyway I stepped inside and had a most kind and wonderful compliment from the young man. He told me. Well! In his words, "I have not seen you before, "You are very pretty, and do you work here?" For a few moments, but only a few, I did not like the compliment as my Uncle always told me 'Iffee get den you ave' ee' give back' (meaning, if you get a compliment, then you might be expected to give a favour back) So I was a little worried, but my new admirer soon put me at my ease. It wasn't long before my friend Margaret was asking for me, and so I had to say my "Goodbyes" and leave the young soldier. For the first time that day I wished that I had an excuse not to go to the meeting. But as the saying goes 'All good things have to come to an end' So I left my new found friend and set off with Margaret and her dad to down town Kingston. The church was packed mainly with young people and we settled ourselves in to the last few remaining seats. A young man was speaking from the platform and that was all I remembered, because my good intention of enjoying the evening had taken a swift turn, and my heart mind and soul was taken over by the meeting of the youthful English soldier from Up Park Camp. The meeting seemed to drag on and on and I wanted to get back to the School to catch a glimpse of him. When I did arrive back, the dormitory it was in darkness. I stood at my window looking across to where he had been. And my deepest wish was to see him step out in to the bright moonlight night. I made plans in my head and in my heart to go over the next morning to see if he would like some breakfast! Of course I would not be so bold but I could dream and wish, there was no harm in that. Well next day I was up earlier than usual, still looking towards the dormitory and hoping I would see him. No such luck, I was tormented, I could not tell anyone in case they wanted to know what I wanted him for. As the days came and went I found my life was taken over by this missing soldier. I tried to counsel myself by saying "I was stupid and should not be feeling like this.

I had lost my appetite and was loosing weight. The girl who I had my meals with was starting to ask questions, like, are you worrying about something? My answer was always "No" but it was clearly not the case. Day in, day out, I dream about this good looking well mannered soldier. Both he and David were missing, and had not been down to the School for some time. There was no one I could talk to about him. Things got so bad that I found myself kneeling at my bedside crying and asking God to take away this feeling of love because he don't even know me. I only saw him for about ten minutes and I am like this. The tears flowed often. Time was passing, and I was just getting myself together and putting behind me the thoughts about the soldier. It was evening and I sat outside in the warm balmy air of the tropical night. The stars were showing off in a blaze of yellow sparkling diamonds. The scent of jasmine was everywhere, the cicadas were calling from the bushes and grass and fireflies (peenies we called them) were flitting to and fro like tiny sunbeams of light, and a soft wind was rustling the tops of the palm trees. I was writing a letter to my Uncle. I heard footsteps. It wasn't Major Wicks, it wasn't the blind school boys, I looked up to see the young soldier I had so desperately been dreaming about. My heart skipped a beat maybe more than once, my mouth open but no words came out. I started trembling and I forced myself to swallow. The young man said "Good evening, writing to you boy friend?" "No" came the reply and I picked up the courage to ask if he had been away? "Yes" came the answer. "We have been away for about two months on hurricane relief work in Honduras and other islands that had been devastated, when Hurricane Hattie" struck the South American Continent and caused many deaths and destruction of property. We were sent off to give aid and help put the island of Anguilla back on its feet. It was very hard but rewarding work" we talked a little more, and then he ask if I had seen David? I pointed him in the right direction, and off he went. I tried to continue my letter to Uncle but just could not concentrate, my head was again in turmoil and my heart was racing. I closed the writing pad and walked to my room. I came back hoping to catch sight of him but he was nowhere to be seen. That night I lay in my bed and was really confused with my thoughts. Oh! He did mention in his conversation that he had written two post cards to me but did not post them because he was worried my handsome big strong boyfriend would beat him up. It was a joke of course and I laughed and told him I had no such boyfriend. And then for the second time he disappeared again. By now I had more self control of my emotions. I was invited to spend the week-end with some senior Blind ladies and was enjoying myself and the occasion. It was time for evening prayers then it was like a sudden bright light bulb exploded in my brain, it was a memory come alive. I had forgotten someone had mentioned that David and the young man, whose name was Michael had taken some of the boys up to the Red Hills for camping over that week-end and they would be bringing them back that night. I quickly thanked everybody for the lovely time I had with them and made up some excuses to leave. They were saying "Don't go yet it is only five o'clock?" Well the bus for Kingston left at 5.30 pm, I could see the confusion on my friend's faces but I could not share this secret. I ran and ran to the bus stop. The bus soon came and I paid my fare and sat back my thoughts intact. There was a Lodge Member who had died during the week, and there was going to be a march at his funeral. What a great excuse for me to get to the front of the School. I knew all the Officers and staff with the children would be out to watch the march past. I was right, for when the band came along; there with the Officers was the man that had caused my heart to be so disrupted! But the old problem started again, no sooner had the band moved on, then everyone started to go back to their places where they had been before, and the soldier had disappeared again. What was I to do now? Do I go to my room and risk not seeing him again or wait? I know what I will do, I told myself, I will run down to my room put some scent on and then come back. I had a very expensive fragrance given to me by an old friend of Uncle's known as 'Daddy' in the local area, a very kind and courteous man. I did not need to put much on for the heady scent filled my room and the air around me. I went back up to the front but no one was there. I sort of hung around and waited. By now the sun was setting and the orange and reds of the sky slowly faded to a velvet blue with the stars putting out their evening show of twinkling glory. I ran down to my room and put some more perfume on, after coming back for the third time it was now after 7pm and clouding over, still no sound of footsteps. Then at last! I could hear the heavy steps of a man, he came around the corner and I was by the School fence. I tried to speak but no sound would come. He was walking away fast, I managed to say "Hello hello" I croaked "Oh! Hello" he said "What are you doing out here"? "Getting some fresh air "I lied. Then without warning the heavens opened up in a typical downpour of torrential rain coming down in grey walls of water. We ran for cover under the porch. Major Wicks ran out to get the children under cover and was shocked to see Michael still at the School. He shouted through the rain "I thought you (Michael) had gone and caught the 7.30pm bus"? Anyway we just stood there under the porch and watched the rain washing the dust of the day down the drive. So we talked and we talked. He did say, he had mentioned to one of the Officers if he could.

# CHAPTER 25

## *My nearly first date.*

Take me out, but was told that the staffs would only pull my leg. I was not at all pleased with that and said "If he wanted to, he can ask me out" So he did, and we made our first date. Oh! I was so excited and happy. What will Uncle think if I told him? All this was going through my mind as we talked. Uncle was a hundred and twelve miles away in Montego Bay so there was no hurry to let him know! And then the rain stopped as suddenly as it had begun. So we said our goodbyes and he left for Up Park Camp with the promise of meeting up later. True to his word he sent me a letter via David. Typical of him David's words were "A letter here from your 'boyfriend" I was sharp in my reply "He is <u>Not</u> my boyfriend" I was worried in case someone from the staffs would overhear, and there would be more nasty remarks from them. It took me a couple of hours to open the letter from Michael for I had to see to my children and get them ready for bed. I was thinking I was in for more disappointment and he wouldn't be taken me to the pictures. I opened his letter in the privacy and quietness of my room.

It was to say that all the soldiers were confined to barracks and on 'Standby for more hurricane 'Relief Duties'. I was a little sad but that I could accept, and wait for another letter or message from David. A few days passed and a message came to meet Michael at the Carib Theatre (A cinema) up at Cross Roads (they were stood down, from Relief Duties) and I had just over a week to wait.

# CHAPTER 26

# Meeting my long lost sister

During that week I had a letter from my Uncle asking if I could come home to Mo' Bay. Two of my brothers had found my missing sister Gloria. After 16½ years. This was a complete shock to me and my mind was in turmoil. I went to the office to see Mrs Captain Wicks. I explained the story and situation to her How Gloria was only about 2 years old when she was snatched away by my Father. I found out that he loved women but could not keep them. My uncle made it clear that my Father did not treat my mother kindly but kept on having his children. My poor Mother had a brain tumour and when she died she was heavily pregnant. My Uncle thought that the doctor took the baby but no one knew for sure. The thinking was that it was better to be with him as there was no one else to look after the newborn child. Time and time again my Uncle ask my father where is Gloria. But he would never give any information about her.

Mrs Wicks always a kind and understanding woman said "You really must go, and meet up with your sister. You will have so much to catch up on." And so I hurriedly packed a few things. Contacted my uncle to say I was coming, and quickly went to the station to catch the train to 'Mo Bay' (Montego Bay) I did have a date with the soldier (Michael) but I thought I would be back in Kingston in plenty of time as it was a week away. My Uncle was there to meet me and we were both excited at the thought of catching up with my long lost sister Gloria, who was also Uncles niece. But it was getting late, and so we had to wait until the next day. It was a Sunday and early that morning my Uncle, brother and myself set out in a taxi to meet my sister. On the way to the parish, my brother told me the story of how they found her. . . . . . . . . . . . . . . . . My two brothers were working on a truck to deliver bananas to an outlying village some 32miles (40km) from Montego Bay. Arriving at the place, they stopped for a break and got talking to a young man who told them there was going to be a dance in the village hall that night and there was a girl who was going to sing and she was good. He asked my brothers if they would like to come but they replied they could not stop as the truck had to be back in 'Mo Bay' (Montego Bay) Anyway after unloading the bananas they thought they might have just enough time to see the young man and possibly hear the girl sing before they left to get back to their depot. At the hall they saw the lad and ask "What was the name of the girl"? And was told it was 'Gloria (Pugh). (That was also the surname of my real father.) So they ask "As she always 'live ere"? And the reply was "Yeh man dat er ouse jus up de road dere" (Sure that's her house just up the road there!) When Gloria appeared to sing, my brothers were shocked and confused. Dat's (Thats) May our sistah? But 'wayt!' (Wait) Mi tawt (thought) Uncle had told us she was in Kingston at the Church. Is 'dis' (This)

Gloria our long lost sistah?? She a look like May. One of my brothers confronted her only to receive a slap round the face He was saying "We tink yu a wi sistah" (We think you are our sister) she shouted back "Ooo are yu? wer you come from? Mi No no yu Mi ave no brudders lef mi alone? (Who are you? Where do you come from? I don't know you, and I have no brothers.) My Brother replied "Yo gat more brudders anna sistah, ere tek dis money and buy sometin" (You have more brothers and a sister, Here take this money and buy something for yourself)

When they arrived back in 'Mo'Bay' they parked the truck and went straight to Uncles to say "Uncle wi a tink wi fine a Gloria" And so it was that we were travelling in the taxi, along a dusty winding country road to meet our long lost sister. At last we arrived and my brother Rasford knocked on the door where Gloria lived. There was a long wait and eventually a very elderly lady opened the door. Rasford explained that he thought Gloria was our sister and we had come to see for ourselves. She said she did not know who the mother or father of Gloria was, but was glad we called, because she had not long to live and thank God that someone came to claim her. Finally Gloria came out to speak to us and I said "Morning Gloria mi am your sistah" (Morning Gloria I am your sister) and a very forceful reply came back "Ow mi no yu a mi sistah"? (How do I know you are my sister?) I replied "Fetcha mirro an look pon de face den ketch a mine" ("Get a mirror and look at your face then look at mine") and with that she broke down and cried and cried. Oh! We had such hugs and cuddles, after all those years and we were finally together again. We promised we would come for her soon.

The next morning I caught the train for Kingston and my mind was in a whirl thinking over the past two days and all that had happened. The train was about sixty miles (96km) from Kingston and slowing down to pull in to a local station, when there was a tremendous screech of metal on metal the carriages rocked and swayed the cases and luggage in the racks came flying down and the train came to a shuddering halt. For a few seconds there was a shocked silence, and then people started to shout and cry out and scramble out of the coaches to see what had happened. . It seemed that the train ran off the line. I was confused and frightened and went to get out. On opening the carriage door, to step out I looked down to see about a 50 foot drop (15.24mtrs) below me. The part of the train I was in was still over a bridge. Dazed and with my head hurting with a knock I had received, I made my way forward to the front part of the train which was actually level with the platform. There were crowds of passengers milling about talking excitedly and a knot of people by the engine. There I saw a man, well, part of a man under the front wheels of the now de-railed train. Nobody seemed to know what had happened?

Eventually news filtered through that we were to wait until the body had been removed and the line was cleared, and some buses were to be sent up from Kingston.

It seemed like a bad dream and to make matters worse I had to get back to meet the young soldier (Michael). The afternoon dragged on and the sun was setting. I watched the police and ambulance and some buses come and go. In those days there weren't many phones around so I couldn't phone the School, but I knew it was on the local radio because the police said so. Those bound for Kingston including me was taken to a waiting bus, I knew by then I had lost my date. I arrived back in Kingston thoroughly fed up. I was thinking I should have caught a taxi and get to Cross Roads to see if Michael was still there? However it wasn't to be, for as I walked out of the station gates, there was Mrs Captain Wick and a couple of the others who came to see if I was alright, and comfort me. On arriving back at the School Mrs Wicks told me to go down to my room, have a shower and get in to bed and she would bring me a tray of food. I tried to protest and say I was O.K but it was no use. She was quite firm in her instructions and after all she was the 'Boss' Oh! I could not sleep, I could not rest. Had I lost him forever? He wouldn't have known about the crash and why I had not turned up for our date. What was I to do? For a couple of weeks I was confused and I could not speak to anyone about it. I finally picked up the courage and ask one of the officers if she could speak to the camps and ask for Bandsman Michael and explain I did not stand him up by choice. I was beside her when they got him to the phone and she just said "I was alright" and put the phone down!! Oh! How could she be so stupid?? Time passed and I really was getting desperate. Now one of the senior girls called Verona worked on the switch board at the Church headquarters in downtown Kingston, I had to explain to her all that had happened and how I was still trying to get in contact with Michael. What a lovely girl, she managed to phone him and told him everything that had gone on, when she got back to the School that night I was anxiously waiting to see if she had managed to speak to him? With A big beam on her face she said "He wants to meet you at the Carib (Cinema). Joy at last! I ask Veronica not to tell the others as I would only be talked about and teased. She was a lovely girl, very kind and caring to the other girls and well loved by all.

I arrived at the Carib promptly at 7.30pm in my best party dress and feeling great. My first date, I was so happy and felt very special. I think I must have a little of the 'Kerr's Pride' as my uncle used to call me 'The Queen'. When the men came to play Dominoes and Cards he use to say "Mine yo' language de Queen is ere" which I think is self explanatory.

# CHAPTER 27

## *What a difference a suit makes?*

Time slowly passed outside the cinema, people came and went inside. I waited and waited Oh! Please let him turn up. A car pull up, someone got out, my heart skip a beat but no, the car pull away and it wasn't Michael. My heart was sinking what was I going to do? Then I look across the road and could not believe my eyes. There he was, so smart and erect as only a soldier could be. I had not recognised him in his suit and he had not recognised me as I had my glasses on and he had never seen me in glasses before. We finally met and laugh at the funny side of the mix up. We were late for the show so Michael suggested we take a taxi to another cinema. We got our tickets and went in. There were a lot of Europeans in the section where we sat. There a lot of stares and 'blue eyes rolling in our direction. (Disapproving Looks!) Michael saw that I was shaking. He thought I was cold (The cinema was air conditioned) but for me it was nerves. We got settled in our seats but I was still shaking. I said "I would be back" and left for the toilets. Oh! I could not stop 'wee-ing' it was my nerves again. I was away for ages; when I got back

Michael ask if I was alright? And he gave me his jacket to put around my shoulders, still thinking I was cold. After the film (A war story set in Korea) we went to find a quick drink of cola and then a taxi back to the school. When we arrived at the school gates, I thought 'here we go I'm not going to be ask out again because I was so long in the toilets' You can imagine my joy when he said "If we could meet again"? I quickly said "Yes" and slipped inside the gates. Sandy, the officer's dog started barking. The lights went on and someone was coming to the balcony to see what the commotion was about. I hurriedly walked down to my room. I was on a high! I felt so happy and so many things were going through my head.

I had been offered a job in Bermuda as a housekeeper, and with all the problems I had encountered with the staffs at the school I could get away to a fresh start. But now I had met this kind considerate and caring man it was a pulling my emotions in both directions, what was I to do? I did not want to get too settled with Michael because the Bermuda offer seemed very tempting and yet my head was always thinking about him. Time passed and an official looking envelope arrived for me, and it was my Passport. Oh! I was so excited I could now get away, but what about Michael? What was I to do? By now we had been seeing one another for some months and I knew I was in love with him. And I felt too he had something in his heart for me. I will have to tell him about the arrival of my Passport. When we met again the weather was overcast and threatening rain, the air was hot and humid. Lightning flickered in long streaks against the background of Long Mountain (North of Kingston) and the rumble of thunder could be heard across the city. He asked in his usual cheerful way "Hello you look very happy tonight? With a deep breath I replied "I am, my Passport arrived this week, so I can now go to Bermuda. His face drop and he said "Oh so you will be happy to leave me"? I explained I was excited in one way but sad in another.

"Eventually you will be going back to England and back to your family and relatives and I might never get this chance again". I never expected to hear what came next when Michael who now became very serious said "Look I don't really want to lose you, so let us get engaged?" And just like the first night when we made our first date, the heavens opened and the rain came thundering down in a solid grey wall of water.

By then we were on our way to tell my very good friend Miss Sewell the exciting news of our forthcoming engagement. Only this time we ran holding hands and laughing (Oh I love the rain) arriving at Miss Sewell house (dripping wet) we told her the news, she laugh, clapped her hands and congratulated both Michael and myself. She offered to go with us to a friend's jewellery shop the following Saturday to get a ring. Oh! I was so excited. Later, when we got back to the School and I was dropped off by taxi. Then nervous reality set in, and to my horror I felt as if I was bursting, and couldn't hold my "Wee" any longer. I started 'wetting' myself just inside the School gates. It trickled down my leg and ran like 'rain water' down a little slope that led out to the road. I fled down the School yard and Horrors! Only to be stopped by Officer out doing the rounds. She ask "If I had a good evening" I mumbled something like "Yes Thank you" and quickly made my way down to my room.

# CHAPTER 28

# The engagement

Michael had to tell the army authorities that he was getting engaged with the intention of marrying me as soon as possible. Now this didn't go down well with the military and he was told that they needed to see me and explain the ups and down that an army wife would encounter. An appointment was made and I had a letter asking me to come to Up Park Camp and meet the Adjutant. I remember I caught the bus up to the camp, Michael was waiting for me and I had a pass to be allowed in. I was trembling and felt many eyes on me as I walked through to the Headquarters building. It seemed a busy place and soldiers were passing by, and going from office to office. Some staring curiously at me some with a big smile as they went past. Eventually I was called by a tall smart looking man with incredibly piercing blue eyes that seemed to read in to your very soul. He politely asked me in to his office, while Michael had to wait outside. He offered me a chair and started to tell me all about the army moves that soldiers had to do. Michael could be away for long periods of time. He could be sent off to a war zone or anywhere. How would I manage in England on my own or other parts of the world while he is away? He was very well-mannered but in his courteous way he was trying to put me off getting married. I explained that Michael had already told me what would be expected when we get married and I was prepared to support him in all that he had to do. He then asked when were we thinking of getting married and I said June. He apologised and said that was not possible as the Army Authorities had to do background checks on Michael to see if he was not already married. Or had a criminal record? It would probably take between three and four months to complete. When I said "That will be fine" He seemed to relax and realise I was not pregnant or pushing to get an English passport. We did not realise at the time but it was the Army's policy to discourage overseas or mixed marriages. He shook my hand and wished me well. Michael was in the Regimental Band and had to go and see the Bandmaster. He called him in to his office and started to say how it wouldn't work. He quoted from a poem by Rudyard Kipling saying "'East is East and West is West and never the twain shall meet" he also said "The girls over here are like flowers in hot houses, once taken out they wither and die' and other nasty remarks from a supposedly educated man. He also said to Michael "Be it on your own head and I will not expect an invite to your wedding" And yet looking back on our wedding photographs he is pictured in many. Michael out of courtesy invited him to our special day. Oh! The time dragged so slowly before I could meet up with Michael and Miss Sewell to choose a ring; but the day did arrive and my stomach was churning with nerve. Anyway we got to the shop and the attendant came with the tray as they were expecting us. I finally found one that I liked and it fitted well. The ring was brought and then we left. I was so happy and excited. During the evening we had already made plans to go out for a meal to celebrate. Before we left, we called in to see (Then) Captains Mr and Mrs Wicks and had my ring blessed (A wonderful thing to do, because I have had so many blessing since). We took a taxi and headed out to the 'Outdoor Restaurant' we had chosen which was at a district called Papine in the hills north of Kingston. The air was cool and sweet. Peeony's (Fireflies) were sparkling like miniature moonbeams all around us. There was a gentle rustling of the palm fronds as they swayed to and fro in the balmy night air.

The stars seemed to shine with an extra polished brilliance against a soft velvet blue of an evening sky. The cicadas were chirruping in the nearby bushes and the frogs were croaking out their mating calls in the hope of attracting a beautiful girl frog or a handsome 'prince' frog. It was the perfect setting to a perfect evening. The waiter was quick and attentive and the meal itself was done to perfection. All too quickly the evening drew to an end. A taxi was ordered, and I headed back to the School and Michael back to the camp. During the meal Michael confided in me by saying his father said, just as he was leaving for Jamaica "Good bye son, look after yourself and don't bring back a 'Black Girl'"!! He said he assured his father that he had no intention of bringing back a 'Black Girl'. In the 1960's prejudice and racial suspicion was very strong. Michael had no prejudices but mentioned that his father was a strict disciplinarian. He said he would write a letter to his Dad letting him know about the engagement and it would be nice to have his approval. I was in daze; my life was going to take a new direction and thoughts tumbled through my head as I tossed and turned in my bed. Did God send Michael to Jamaica especially for me? No one apart from my uncle Ivan showed me such love and care? Will his dad, auntie's sisters, cousin and grandmother accept me? Will I like England and its cold frosty weather? What about the food would I like it? I laid there in the dark in my little room unable to sleep. The hours slipped by and the morning eventually came. I sat up with a start, had I fallen asleep and dreamt it all? No there it was my bright shiny new engagement ring on my finger to remind me this was for real. It was time to get up and rouse the children still sleeping in the dormitory and get them ready for the day. The practice was to roll back the bedclothes. Teeth to be cleaned, Send some to the class rooms for dusting and tidying duties. There were shoes and socks to be matched, hair to comb and uniforms to be neatly sorted. Remember all the children were blind but they were used to this routine. I had to make sure they were at the dining room on time for morning grace and breakfast. Then back to the dormitory for a last brushing of teeth and a final room and uniform inspection before assembly and the start of school. My mind still being in a whirl I cannot remember what was said about the engagement in assembly when it was announced to the whole school. The children of course were very excited and although without sight they said they could see it coming for a long time.

I knew I would have to face the staffs and their nasty comments and as I expected cruel things were said but many and wanted to see my ring so more criticism could heaped on me. One day I was helping the children with the washing up and I took off my ring and placed it on the window ledge. It was only for a short time but when I look around my ring was gone. I was so VERY ANGRY. I stormed up to the dining hall where Mrs. Wicks was working, I explained what had happened and she said she would have to search the staff room lockers. I went back down to where I had been with the children and told the staffs what was going to happen and the next thing I knew my ring had been put back. I sort of knew who had taken it. The Cook, Miss Peel. I was told by others that she had been seeing a 'Obeah Woman' as they say in Jamaica. A (Clairvoyant or witch doctor) that lived in Spanish Town (The Old Capital City of the island) she had to take something personal of mine and take to the 'Obeah Woman' so she could work her magic. The original idea was to get rid of me from working at the school. I found out later there was a much more sinister motive.

Oh! God has blessed me, I am the happiest and most fulfilled person on earth. Do I ever stop thinking about the next step which was the wedding? How do I start? I was not the sort of person to talk things over with friends and I was always cautious about sharing personal problems as I had so many setbacks when dealing with people. But the wedding preparations were on my mind. I was so sure that my eldest uncle's wife would make my wedding dress, I was very excited. A few weeks later after our engagement I went to see her but as I found with people, she told me she would not make it. I thought she would be happy for us, especially for me as I used to live with her, and worked very hard without any pay. Her reply was a blunt "No". I was shocked; I had very little money and not a very helpful family.

# CHAPTER 29

# Wedding preparations

A few days later I was speaking to an elderly lady (Mrs Jones) who did sewing for the children at the Church School. I told her about the wedding dress I would like, but only had limited funds. She laughed and said she would bring a pattern she had from America for me to see. Oh! I was overjoyed. A few days later I was looking at a beautiful picture of the 'Perfect Wedding Dress'. I could not believe my eyes, and God had answered my prayers. She told me I would need a second dress which she will also make. Life for me had taken on a new meaning. I went to see Mrs. Major Wicks for my savings and knew straight away the money would not go very far, but enough to get two sets of material and trimmings for both. One was white with small red roses in the frills and the other was yellow with a black velvet cummerbund and rind stones. So I was set for that 'Special Day' in October 21$^{st}$ 1961. That date had been resting in my heart for months and as they slipped by, the planning and preparations seem to come quicker and quicker. But still there was no news from Michael's dad. Every time we met I would ask "Have you heard anything from your father? The answer was always "Not yet" Then one day Michael appeared with a big grin on his face and a rather fat letter in his hand. It was from his dad and more than that it was from his sisters as well. His father said he would welcome Lilly May (Me) as his future daughter in law and hoped we would settle in to the family. He then sent his reply on to Michael's sisters who then added their comments to the letter. Stella, Jean and Brenda said very much the same that they would be looking forward to meeting me and having a new sister in law and hoped I would be very happy with Michael in England. Then the letter was sent back to him.

Captain and Mrs. Wicks took on most of the organising the wedding for which both Michael and I will be ever grateful. They would push me out of the kitchen saying "Don't you worry about a thing it's all taken care of". I even learnt (Later) that they were trying to ice the wedding cake at 4.30 in the morning when the temperature was at its coolest because the icing would not set. They organised the venue, the seating, and the refreshments. They saw to the helpers and servers for our eighty six guests. They arranged the tables and seating. And the many other little bits that made our day so special. No words can ever be enough for gratitude we felt for those two wonderful people. Michael and I went house hunting some months before and found an ideal little place not too far from the camp. The address was 23. Sackville Road. Michael and his soldier friends had been decorating and painting the place for weeks. The owners who were Cubans had a big house just in front of ours, which was raised on concrete stilts that stood about four feet high (roughly 1.50m) so the air would circulate and keep the house cooler. For us, our place was ideal with a bedroom a lounge/dining room a kitchen and a veranda that went the length of the house Again Captain Wicks came to the rescue and arranged for the house to be filled with all the necessary furniture. It was my first house I was so excited and so proud. All was set for our perfect day!!

On the 20th October (The day before our wedding) I had planned in the evening to take some of the senior girls to the house to do the last minute dusting and cleaning.

# CHAPTER 30

# The storm

The day started of dull and grey which was not unusual in October as it was the wettest month in the calendar. The air was heavy and humid with moisture. The thunder was rumbling around Long Mountain again, and it looked all set for rain. It started slowly at first. Big fat droplets which got heavier and heavier and faster and faster until the rain fell with a hiss and then a roar. Buildings at the school were blotted out in a cloudburst of water and soon the streets were awash like rivers.

All the public transport and taxi's stopped running and downtown Kingston was submerged under about two feet of brown and fast flowing water. Oh horrors!! What if the weather was like this tomorrow? I and the senior girls still had to get up to Sackville Road, with no transport we had to walk. So we hitched up our dresses took off our shoes hung them round our necks and waded paddles and squelched the 3 miles (Just under 4.5 Kilometres) to the house. Michael was not there but we had a key and soon the girls familiarised themselves with the lay out and set to with the final tidying up. They are so clever as most of the cleaning was done by feel and touch and the occasional question like, "how were the shelves, or is the veranda swept"? When we had finished we were tired but happy and then had to trek the 3 miles back to the School for the Blind, through streets which were still running with water although not so fast or deep.

Back in my little room I lay in bed wondering how tomorrow would be? My mind was in a whirl, how would my life change? Did Michael truly love me? Was I doing the right thing? Would I be happy in England? So many questions and no answers to convince myself that my life was going to change for the better? I must have dropped off to sleep for the next thing I knew was the sun shining through my window.

I sat up with a start. It was today, Saturday 21st October 1961 the most important day of my life and there was so much to do before the wedding. I had to get my fourteen children up, see them fold their bedclothes properly. The mattresses had to be turned. And their showers to be supervised, everything had to be ready before breakfast. My stomach was in a knot I couldn't face food. I was so anxious about my 'big day', and the final realisation that I would no longer be caring and looking after my dear little girls who had shown me so much love and loyalty. I saw them all off to breakfast then went back to my room to pack my belongings not that were many, and put away my bedding. I kept well away from the staffs as I knew I would be hearing sarcastic and unkind remarks pointed at me again.

Do you remember me mentioning 'Miss Peel' the school cook? Well, I found out much later that she too had got up very early on that day and caught a bus to Spanish Town. (*The old Jamaican Capital*) Where she went to see the Obeah

(Witchcraft) Woman so as to work her magic and curse our wedding. How that woman must have hated me!! I think it was because I was marrying a white man and her daughter who was a teacher, should have been in that position??

Mrs Captain Wicks gave the staffs the afternoon off so there would be no one there to either spoil the food or make nasty comments about me. They were not very pleased about that. What a wise and wonderful woman she was. I think back to that day and knew I received a blessing. The sky was the bluest of blue. Not a cloud in sight. Gone were the dark heavy clouds of yesterday. The sun seemed extra bright and the birds were singing as if they were celebrating with me. The leaves on the trees were polished to perfection and I have never seen grass look so green. The air was sweet with scent of bougainvillea and it seemed the whole world was holding its breath waiting for our wedding to come.

# CHAPTER 31

# The Wedding.

I had to go and get my hair styled and the flowers to pick up and horror!! Who should I see but Michael pedalling down to the Church Hall in downtown Kingston? He did not look too pleased to see me as it was bad luck to see your intended wedding partner before the actual wedding and was rather curt when we spoke. He was off to get changed in to his dress uniform. I was with a friend at the time and was and thinking this is not a good start. My friend seemed rather shocked and was no doubt thinking the same as myself. Anyway I had to get on as I also had to have my dress fitted. Time was racing by and three o'clock was fast approaching. Mrs Jones fitted and dressed me and seemed very pleased with her handiwork. I felt like a queen I had never had or held such a dress and it was a perfect fit. Oh everything was going to be just fine. I heard the blare of a horn outside and it was Mr Lewis with his car ready to take me to Bramwell Booth Memorial Hall where Michael would be there waiting for me.

We sped down town to Kingston as if in a dream and

there was the Army Hall and uncle ready at the steps ready to escort me down the aisle. With uncle holding my arm, I climbed the steps in to the building. I was trembling like a leaf, my stomach was churning and my bouquet was shaking and rustling as if it was in a high wind, until a friend just inside the door said "OH Miss Lilly May you look beautiful" and with that my shaking and rustling stopped. I was so grateful to that girl. I peeped down to the front to see if Michael was there, and sure enough was a pink well scrubbed young man looking very smart in his dress uniform. And alongside him was David his best man. I started down the aisle and felt many eyes on me from the guests and well wishers. As I slowly walked towards him I felt a tug on my arm. It was my Aunty in law (smiling) who had refused to make my wedding dress. I ignored her as she had been so unkind to me. Besides I felt so good in what I was wearing. I was now at the front, facing Captain Nelson the Church Officer who was going to perform the wedding ceremony. It was time to let the past go, Time to forget the pain, suffering and anxieties I went through when growing up. As much as I loved my uncle it was time to let go, and join with Michael in our new life together.

o-o-o-o-o-o-o-o-o-o-o-o-o-o-o-o-o-o-o-o-o

# Epilogue

My story of "Montego May" is nearly over, my future at the time was uncertain.

I can say with hand on heart 'I am truly blessed' in my marriage, our deep and strong love for one another, and of course my family. My story doesn't stop here; it goes on to new and wonderful experiences we share together. But that' is another story to tell!!

I would like to leave you with a poem by Patience Strong which we have kept in our Wedding Album.

> The wedding day is over and you as man and wife
> Set out on your journey, down the winding path of life.
> Facing every kind of weather, fortunes change and chance
> But finding in the great adventure, glory and romance
>
> To the dreams of this high moment true may you remain?
> Whether fate send golden sunshine, storm or cloud or rain.
> May you be unto each other, comrade, sweetheart, friend.
> And good companions on the roadway, faithful to the end.

Lightning Source UK Ltd.
Milton Keynes UK
UKOW04f0150190717
305594UK00001B/13/P